Praise for *Small Business Finance for the Busy Entrepreneur*

Small Business Finance for the Busy Entrepreneur is the book I wish I had read when I started my business a few years ago. It would have saved me lots of time and money, and lessened the headaches from managing both my personal and business financials. If you're looking to start a business or have been in business for a couple years, read this book to get your financial house in order. Sylvia Inks does an amazing job creating a go-to resource for the busy entrepreneur.

— **Jason Vitug**, founder at Phroogal and bestselling author of *You Only Live Once: The Roadmap to Financial Wellness and a Purposeful Life.*

As someone who considers herself financially-savvy, starting my business after leaving corporate was still an eye-opener. If I had read Sylvia's book, I would have saved even more money and a lot of time figuring out how best to organize and manage the financial side of my business. This book is a very valuable investment. It's never too late to get started on the right financial path for business success.

— **Marcey Rader**, Productivity and Health Coach, bestselling author of *Beyond Travel: A Road Warrior's Survival Guide.*

What can one woman from the technology consulting world teach small business owners about understanding our numbers so we can make wise business decisions and grow our businesses faster? Lots! Sylvia Inks has created the blueprint guide for setting up the right processes, tailored to your specific business situation that may well change both your life and your business!

— **Diana M. Needham**, CEO, Needham Business Consulting

Sylvia Inks has created an important resource for business owners of all types, for entrepreneurs and for students of Business Planning alike. This well-written, well-edited "how to" book provides coverage on a number of important business topics that are not specifically covered in most introductory books on this topic.

— **Jim Joyce**, President, Sales Partners, Inc., Instructor, Coach Business Planning

Small Business Finance for the Busy Entrepreneur really is for everybody that is starting a business or has done so within the last couple of years. In fact *Small Business Finance for the Busy Entrepreneur* is a great book for any small business owner whose business isn't on a solid foundation. I wish this book was available when I started my business. It is practical, pragmatic, clear, and full of examples and "how to" forms. It will get added to my list of "must read books" for my clients.

— **Bill Davis**, Business Coach and Owner, Team Nimbus of North Carolina

Working daily with small business owners, I see firsthand many of the mistakes that they make in not focusing on establishing and running their business in the correct manner. Sylvia's book is a great instruction manual for anyone who is looking to start their own business, or anyone who already has a business and is bogged down with disorganization and inefficiency. Her recommendations to rely on professionals like CPAs, attorneys, and financial advisors is spot on.

— **John Ashby Ware**, ChFC, CLU, CExP, President, Ware Financial Partners *www.warefinancialpartners.com*

Not managing their numbers is why many small businesses fail. *Small Business Finance for the Busy Entrepreneur* gives sound business tips all entrepreneurs need to know to organize their business finances.

— **Jess R. McLamb**, President, Roper Bookkeeping/ Roper Strategies

While I wish I had this book five years ago, I am more ready now than ever before, to follow the very simple steps and action items in *Small Business Finance for the Busy Entrepreneur.* I found the case studies provided an additional way to understand the basic concepts, inspiring me to make thoughtful decisions ... and that it's never too late! Thank you Sylvia Inks for this work. I'm grateful and so will many be.

— **Leslie Flowers**, Managing Member, Leslie Flowers Enterprises LLC

SMALL BUSINESS FINANCE FOR THE BUSY ENTREPRENEUR

Blueprint for Building a Solid, Profitable Business

By Sylvia Inks

SMALL BUSINESS FINANCE FOR THE BUSY ENTREPRENEUR.
Blueprint for Building a Solid, Profitable Business

ISBN: 978-0-9980518-0-2
Library of Congress Control Number: 2016914793
Cover Design by Nathanial Dasco.

The publisher has strived to be as accurate and complete as possible in the creation of this book.

This book is not intended for use as a source of legal, business, accounting, tax, or financial advice. All readers are advised to seek services of competent professionals in legal, business, accounting, tax, and financial fields.

In practical advice books, as in anything else in life, there are no guarantees of income made. Readers are cautioned to rely on their own judgment about their individual circumstances and to act accordingly.

While all attempts have been made to verify information provided for this publication, the publisher assumes no responsibility for errors, omissions, or contrary interpretation of the subject matter herein. Any perceived slights of specific persons, peoples, or organizations are unintended.

Names, locations and types of businesses associated with illustrative stories in this book have been changed to protect the privacy of individuals and businesses.

Dedication

The book is dedicated to my husband, Greg, who encouraged me to follow my passion and start my own business.

To all aspiring entrepreneurs and small business owners: May this book provide you the knowledge to make your business a profitable success!

Acknowledgements

Thank you Diana M. Needham, my book marketing coach, for believing in me and in the message that I wanted and needed to share with the world.

Thank you to Leslie Flowers, my editor, for polishing this book with her "gold standard of editing" skills. I will be forever grateful that the timing worked out perfectly for you to take on this project.

Thank you to Paggy Wu, my accountability partner, who has been there for me from the very beginning of this journey when my business was just an idea.

Thank you to Elizabeth Corgan Powell, who provided the creative input at the early design of the company.

Thank you to Beth Lavin, who has always been there for me when I needed her the most -- to celebrate the wins and to share in the chaos.

Thank you to my entrepreneur teacher and mentor, Jim Joyce, who taught me the fundamentals of business planning and customer needs.

Thank you to Bill Davis for the invaluable lesson on calculating the yield per hour.

Thank you to my legal, accounting, and tax colleagues for helping to review the accuracy of the manuscript. Thank you to all the generous people who read my manuscript to provide feedback, real-life stories, and endorsements. A special thank you to Jess R. McLamb, Calley Gerber, Marcey Rader, Ashby Ware, Kathleen Anckner, Helen Moses, Wendy Gates Corbett, and Lily Keyes who went above and beyond in providing the feedback to get this book to the level of quality and accuracy needed.

Thank you to all my current and former clients who trusted me with their hopes, fears, and financial challenges. You are my inspiration for writing this book.

Thank you to my husband Greg and two young boys – who supported me as I worked to finish this book. I am happy to say that it's done and I look forward to spending more family time together.

And last but not least, thank you to my dad, whose entrepreneurial spirit I inherited. He has taught me that success and money can only be achieved through hard work and calculated risks.

A Special Bonus From SMI Financial Coaching

There are books and free information online on how to manage the information and processes needed to run a profitable business, yet in this book I provide all the key topics in one place to give you a great starting point to minimize hours searching for and obtaining this information in various places.

As a special bonus for buying this book, I've created templates to help you get started with getting your arms around your business finances. As an additional bonus, you'll also have access to a resource page with links to not only the resources (companies, software programs, and other resources) mentioned in this book, but also to new tools, technologies, and programs I discover and recommend.

Go to www.smallbusinessfinancebook.com/kit to sign up for access to your bonus material.

As another special gift, I'll also be sending tips, tricks, and great information to make your life easier around your business finances.

Let's get started!

Sylvia

Table of Contents

Introduction

The yellow moving truck rolled up to the driveway on an early Saturday morning, as I am still drinking my first cup of coffee. I watched the movers pack up the last of their belongings. I am happy to see these business owners, who have become like family to me, move forward and try to make the best of the situation, but I am still shocked that it had finally come to this ...

Six months earlier ...

Returning home from a grueling twelve-hour workday filled to the brim with back-to-back client meetings, I notice two banker's boxes stacked in front of my front door. I had a sinking feeling that these people — the ones I cared so much about — were on the brink of losing everything. I knew I had a long night ahead of me and was certainly not prepared for what was to come over the next few weeks.

After two weeks of working until 2:00 am to go through bank statements, credit card statements, and outstanding bills, I saw that these business owners had commingled their personal and business assets and were borrowing from the business to pay for their mortgage and groceries. From the outside, these two college-educated graduates, owners of an engineering consulting business, both making over $100,000 in sales each year and living in a three-story house, appeared to be rich. They had a CPA advising them on a monthly basis for what they should be doing; however, after carefully reviewing their bank and credit card accounts, I found that one of their employees had embezzled funds over a period of months and they were at risk of bankruptcy along with IRS penalties and fines if audited.

As I watched this whole scenario unravel, I will tell you this: there were knots in my stomach. I felt like I was going to throw up, because I saw what was going to happen to these people that I really cared about and I felt like there was nothing that could change their outcome. It would only be a matter of time before they were forced to foreclose on their home, unless circumstances didn't change immediately. I felt the burden of responsibility and took it upon myself to try to salvage their personal and business situation. At least I could try.

This was a very emotional and stressful time for all of us. Based on my recommendations, these two business owners sold their three-story house and moved into a two-bedroom apartment. After a year of saving, minimizing expenses, and paying off debt, they bought their dream retirement home by the ocean. Unfortunately, two years later, more significant financial issues arose, and they used up all their life savings in less than six months ... which they had incorrectly thought would last at least ten years. With the stress of not knowing how they would survive and pay for food and a roof over their heads, they swallowed their pride and asked for help. They made phone calls to family members and sheepishly asked for money to solve their cash flow issue. With only two out of five family members agreeing to give them money, their anger at the other three family members caused a strain in the relationship that was never repaired. Despite the monetary gifts, they were unable to save their business; they closed their business, sold their dream retirement home, and started over again.

I learned from this experience that having a college degree and being great in math does not guarantee the skills to be successful in running your own profitable business. Also, having a CPA that tells you what to do doesn't matter if you don't actually follow the advice! How many times have you attended classes, workshops, and webinars aimed at helping you get your arms around your business finances, yet, left the training still confused, overwhelmed, and even a bit afraid whenever you thought about the numbers in your business?

Even though I was a highly paid consultant inside the financial services industry for ten years, when I started my own financial coaching business, I quickly realized that I didn't know *what I didn't know*. I went to small business seminars to learn about key topics including bookkeeping, accounting, business loans, marketing, and social media. It is easy to spend more hours than you intended while searching the Internet, attending classes, and reading books to find the answers to your small business finance questions. After all my research, I met with my CPA to verify a list of questions. Despite my research and concise list of questions, the meeting went over the allotted hour. Knowing that I was being billed at $210 per hour, I was getting increasingly anxious and worried about the bill as time ticked away ... and we finished two hours later!

After investing hundreds of hours and thousands of dollars on various training, seminars, and paid professionals over the last several years, I know one thing for sure ... the information required to start and run a profitable small business cannot be found in one place. I wrote this book to share with you — in one place — the key lessons I have learned, real-life stories, and information that I had gathered during my first year in business experience ... so you can save yourself time, money, and stress. It is easy to spend hours searching the Internet, attending classes, and reading books. As a small business owner, time is precious, especially if you are starting this on the side or juggling family responsibilities. You can also spend more money than is necessary consulting with CPAs and business lawyers if you do not know what to ask before those meetings.

Here's a statistic that breaks my heart: According to the U.S. Small Business Administration, over 50% of small businesses shut down within the first five years[1]. Many don't make it past the first eighteen months. Most of the reasons why they fail are things that could have been easily avoided. This is the heart of why I started my financial coaching business – to empower small business owners to succeed and maintain that success and their livelihood. Small businesses are the backbone of our economy. I admire those individuals who have the dedication and drive to start their own business. Let's increase your chances of financial success by taking smart actions!

Inside this book you will find many things you likely have already heard or read somewhere that you should do. However, time may have gotten in the way, you didn't know exactly how or where to start, or you didn't really see why it was important ... not then, that is. What's different about this book is that there are real-life stories to show why these things are important, detailed examples to understand how calculations were made, and templates to show you how to get started on your own. With access to my bonus section, you will be able to save time by downloading ready-to-use templates and access resources mentioned in this book.

Who This Book is For

If you are an entrepreneur, and you are not making the profits that you want and need in the business, don't fully understand the numbers in running your business, and are wishing you could get a handle on the finances in order to spend more time with your family, this book is for you. If you know a struggling small business owner or have a spouse who is working too many late nights on the business, please purchase this book to show them there is a blueprint for building a solid, profitable business.

I wrote this book primarily for the small business owners, offering their own products and services. They are sole proprietors, single-member LLCs, or multi-member LLCs (who did not elect S-Corp). They are great at what they do, yet aren't good with numbers. They are financially stressed, overwhelmed, and frustrated with piles of paperwork and high tax bills. Most of these small businesses have only one person working on the business (the entrepreneur/owner), and are looking and wanting to expand their team to accommodate business growth. They have been in business for at least one year and know that they don't know everything they need to know to run a profitable, successful business.

Direct Sales Representatives and Independent Consultants

Many of my direct sales clients and colleagues have shared that their companies are great at training them on how to sell the products, but don't give any training on how to manage the paperwork, processes, and finances to running their "own business." For example, one of my direct sales clients said that the steps and templates that I provided during our small business coaching sessions was going to save her over twenty hours in tax preparation this year.

You may conclude that some chapters may not apply to you. I encourage you, however, to at least briefly skim them as you may find that there are different, more efficient ways to save time, money, and frustration based on the tips and client examples. I have written this book so that each chapter can be read alone, so you can first jump to the chapters that most pertain to your current business challenges, and then go back and read the book in its entirety.

Full Disclaimer: I am not a CPA or business lawyer.

This book is not to meant to replace tax or legal advice from a licensed professional. I did seek advice from these professionals when writing this book to make every effort to ensure the information contained in this book is accurate.

Many of the books and sites, including IRS.gov that I referenced when starting my business, were complex. For someone who likes numbers, spreadsheets, and software, even I had a hard time following some of these forms. With my business degree and IT professional consulting background, focused on process improvements for many Fortune 500 companies, I created a practical, easy-to-understand guide that gives you a starting point to understand what questions you should ask and what areas you need to cover with these professionals. I have also included stories and examples to make the material more relatable and show you how to incorporate the advice in each chapter.

I am a firm believer that knowledge is power. This book will help you understand what you don't know and create a system and process that works for you to best maximize your success as a small business owner.

How to get the most out of this book.

1. **If you are just starting your business or you are so overwhelmed that you need to start with a clean slate** – this is the perfect time to read this book! Start reading from the beginning to end, as the chapters are presented in a logical, progressive order of what you should do to create a successful business. There are four parts to this book. The first set of chapters help you "build a solid foundation" for your business. The second set of chapters help you understand the steps to "construct solid walls and infrastructure" so that your business doesn't easily fall apart. The third set of chapters explains how to "protect your business with a strong roof." The last chapter is how to "make improvements."
2. **If you are an existing small business owner with several years of experience or looking to see what you can improve** – review the table of contents and jump straight to those chapters to get help and solve your most burning pains and questions right away. Then, go back through and read the book in its entirety, especially sections that you may not be 100% sure that you are doing the most effectively or efficiently. Even if you think you have a topic covered, check it out, as there are helpful tips that many seasoned business professionals who have been in business for years have learned, that they are not doing correctly.

Part I:

Build a Solid Foundation

"It is not the beauty of a building you should look at; it's the construction of the foundation that will stand the test of time."
— David Allan Coe

Chapter 1

Separate Personal and Business Expenses

One of the most important things you can do as a small business owner is to separate your business from your personal finances. According to a 2015 TD Bank survey[2], 56% of small business owners use their checking for both business and personal expenses. When you commingle the two, you can waste hours trying to sort through bank and credit card transactions, spend more money for taxes and CPA fees, and open yourself to an IRS nightmare. If you want to save time, have more money, and pay fewer taxes, take the time to open business bank accounts and associated credit cards to keep your personal and business dollars separate.

What You Need

- Tax Identification Number (TIN) – also known as Employer Identification Number (EIN) for registered businesses.
- Legal paperwork with registered business name.
- Business Checking Account (1) – to pay for business expenses.
- Business Savings Account (minimum of 2) – the first one for tax savings and the second for future savings/investment purchases .

  (More information for why you need a tax savings account in Chapter 6: Make Tax Day Less Stressful.)
- Business Credit Card (1) – to pay for business expenses.

Tip - It takes less than 15 minutes to apply for and receive an Employer Identification Number (EIN). It's also free at IRS.gov! Don't get scammed by sites that charge a fee to give you a tax identification number.

Direct Sellers and Independent Contractors

If you are hired and are doing business under your own personal name, and you are treated as a sole proprietor for tax purposes, then you are likely using your social security number (SSN) as your tax identification number (TIN). To protect your personal identity and build your business brand, apply for an Employer Identification Number (EIN) to avoid giving out your social security number. You can also register for a "Doing Business As" (DBA) Name, which is a fictitious name that is different from your personal name. *(See Chapter 16: Protect Your Family and Business for details for why being a sole proprietor is not the best financial decision.)*

When you have separate bank accounts and credit cards, then use the business credit card and bank accounts only for business purposes. Same goes for personal credit card and bank accounts – only use those for personal expenses. You should always avoid using your personal credit card to pay for a business expense. Similarly, avoid using your business credit card to pay for personal items. Even if you are a sole proprietor, by having a DBA, you can keep everything separate and have dedicated business accounts and credit cards.

If you *overlooked* a business expense that was paid for by your personal credit card, the unfortunate result is that you lose out on claiming that business deduction. In other words, **you paid *more* taxes than you really owed**. Separate accounts help you to be sure you are deducting all eligible business expenses, which will save you both time and money.

More importantly, **if you *incorrectly* claimed a business expense**, that was truly a personal item, there may be ugly consequences if you are audited by the IRS. That means **you paid *fewer* taxes than you owed.** This is an easy mistake to do when you commingle funds. Regardless of whether it was an oversight or purposeful, the government slaps a penalty and calculates interest starting from the date you should have paid. That could mean interest that is calculated back from three to five years!

Now that you understand the importance of having dedicated bank accounts, the next question is where to open your checking and savings accounts? There are several key factors to take into consideration, including convenience, fees, and balance requirements.

Out of convenience, you may think it is easier, and logically better to open your business checking and savings account where your personal accounts are located. Opening a new business account where you already have personal accounts can cut the amount of time to set-up in half. On the other hand, community banks usually give small business owners the best rates, lower fees, and lower minimum balance requirements. National banks have higher balance requirements so if you don't keep that specific balance each month to waive the account fees, the monthly maintenance fees can cost us upwards of $200 or more per year!

If you travel for business and will need bank access, having your accounts at a community bank may not be your best solution. Decide based on what is best for you and your business and find out first if there are branches in your travel locations. Otherwise, you can use your business debit and credit card if you are making purchases during your travel and do not need teller and banking assistance.

Are you thinking, "In theory separating the business and personal finances is the right thing to do, but there are exceptions, right?" There are no exceptions. You must keep them separated. Period.

Commonly asked questions if you are thinking, there may be exceptions.

1. **What if I haven't officially started my business and am still in the planning phases?**

   If you are serious about starting and owning a business, you should make everything official from the beginning. Decide on and then register the business name, form your legal entity, apply for an EIN, and open the three business banking accounts.

   When opening your bank accounts, be sure to bring all the necessary paperwork, including the tax identification number (recommend EIN, not SSN), the legal paperwork with registered business name, driver's license, social security number, and a second form of identification, such as a passport.

   When you are spending money for start-up expenses, dedicate one credit card to use for these start-up costs. Then when your CPA asks you for a tally of the start-up expenses, you can pull statements from just that one credit card and be 100% confident that you haven't missed any possible expenses that can be claimed for business purposes. That one credit card should only have been used for items to start-up the business.

	*Tip - Save yourself time in finding and claiming all of your business deductions by having a dedicated business credit card for business expenses.*

2. **What if there's not enough cash in the business account and I need to purchase inventory for the business?**

   If you need to use personal money because the business isn't generating enough income yet, you still keep everything separate. First, decide if the personal funds going into the business will be treated as equity (i.e., an investment) or as a loan that the business needs to repay. If you are a sole proprietor or your business is a limited liability company (LLC), money invested into the business is called *owner's equity* or *member's equity*. Otherwise, if you want the money to be a loan, be sure to keep track of the dates and amounts of all loans so they can be repaid in the future.

   Then, you write the business a personal check or transfer money from your personal checking account into your business checking account.

	*Tip: Make sure you keep a running total of cash deposits to show your CPA when money should be designated as owner's investment or members' investments, NOT income from the business.*

3. **What if I'm at the store and I need to purchase both business and personal items?**

   Separate the items into two piles and ask the cashier to ring up two separate transactions, using your personal credit card for your personal items and your business credit card for the business items. This same concept is applied for online purchases as well.

CASE STUDIES

I want to share three real-life stories from clients and colleagues who did not keep personal and business expenses separate, and ended up having to pay a bookkeeper and CPA for help:

1. **Small business owner who mixed business and personal expenses.**

   Sara S. came to me for help to increase her cash flow as she was living paycheck-to-paycheck and needed to make more money in her landscaping design business. Unfortunately, she had already agreed to pay a bookkeeper $800 to sort through nine months of bank transactions where she had commingled personal with business banking. The bookkeeper had to manually go through and flag items that seemed questionable, including ATM withdrawals of various amounts. Then Sara had to go through and try to recall if it was a business purchase or an owner's draw. As the owner, she was the only person who could say whether something was a business expense or not. But that's not all. Later, she was subjected to an IRS audit and decided to hire an accountant to help her because she was overwhelmed. She spent well over a thousand dollars in her first year of business hiring others to fix her finances. All of this could have been easily avoided by taking an hour to open separate accounts when she first began her business.

2. **Small Business Owner and the "data dump" of an entire year's worth of bank transactions to CPA.**

   Chris P., a CPA at a large accounting firm, told me that one of his small business clients sent Chris an Excel file with downloaded bank transactions for the entire year to have him prepare taxes. It took Chris four hours to sort through 10,000 transactions and separate the business from personal transactions. At a bill rate of $200 per hour, this business owner paid an additional $800 in tax preparation fees due to not having opened separate accounts at the start. That was hard-earned money spent by the client for something that was completely avoidable had the client maintained separate accounts.

3. **Small Business Owner who put business expenses on a personal credit card.**

   Melanie C., a broker at a large realty company, shared with me that she completely forgot to analyze one of her personal credit cards that was used for business expenses when having her CPA prepare her taxes. Two days before the April 15th deadline, she realized her oversight and sent her business expenses to the CPA. He had already completed the tax return and had to re-do it, charging Melanie an additional $200 in tax preparation fees for the time spent having to recalculate taxes.

Summary

It is important to separate your personal and business finances to save time, money, and stress. While you may have originally thought that you don't need to do this until the business is making money, you now know that it will cost more time and money in the long-term to have a bookkeeper or CPA sorting through the expected mess. Other consequences could include 1) paying a tax penalty because you incorrectly claimed something as a business expense, and/or 2) paying more in taxes because you missed an expense to claim as a business deduction. Separating accounts can save you hundreds and possibly thousands of dollars each year.

Refer to the following template to help you research several community and national banks to decide where to open your business checking and savings accounts.

For links to resources and ready-to-use templates referenced in this chapter, visit www.smallbusinessfinancebook.com/kit and enter your email address to gain instant access.

Template: Research for Bank Accounts

Business Checking				
Bank Name				
Type of Account				
Monthly Maintenance Fee				
Average Monthly Balance Required				
How to Avoid Monthly Maintenance Fee				
No. of Transactions Included				
Minimum Opening Balance				

Business Savings				
Bank Name				
Type of Account				
Monthly Maintenance Fee				
Average Monthly Balance Required				
How to Avoid Monthly Maintenance Fee				
No. of Transactions Included				
Minimum Opening Balance				

Decisions Made:

Opened Accounts at: ______________________________[banking institution(s)]

Business checking (for operating expenses): _______________ (last 4 digits of account number)

Business savings (for tax savings): _______________ (last 4 digits of account number)

Business savings: _______________ (last 4 digits of account number)

Chapter 2

Predict Your Financial Success

If you jump into starting your own business without taking the time to define your ideal customer and financial plan, you ***can and likely will waste a lot of time and end up frustrated.*** By doing your research upfront, you can increase the chances that your business will be successful and achieve a higher return on your investment. While evaluating the numbers may not seem as much fun as making money or feels too complicated for you, it can save you time and money because you know in advance whether your business is viable based on the customers you plan to target. Given that almost 50% of new businesses fail within their first five years[1], take the time to focus on the financial section of your business plan to predict your financial success. Even if you don't need financing, doing a financial forecast will enable you to understand if and when you can make a profit. You may be surprised to learn that your business is not as viable as you think, or that you need to make some drastic changes in order to stay *in* business.

Common mistakes that small business owners make in their business and finances:

- Commingling personal and business expenses so it is unclear how much the business is making or costing.
- Running out of cash before the business takes off.
- Marketing to the wrong customers (i.e., those who can't or aren't willing to pay, or who don't want your products or services now).
- Setting prices too low.

If you thinking that a financial plan sounds too formal, it doesn't have to be complicated, particularly if you are not planning to obtain financing for your business. Your main goal is to understand *start-up expenses* (if you haven't started your business), *cost of goods sold*, *operating expenses* (i.e., rent, equipment, inventory cost), and expected sales over a period of time to determine if you will have a profit or loss. While you may experience losses at the onset of your business or in some slow months, overall, be sure that your business is generating income.

If you don't know if you are making a profit because your personal and business finances are commingled, refer to Chapter 1: Separate the Personal and Business Expenses to learn the best way to create your business accounts.

If you are just starting your business, be sure to research the total start-up expenses when planning your business venture and ensure you have enough cash to cover the bills. If cash is an issue, consider reading Chapter 17: Build A Cash Cushion For Greater Flexibility before you continue.

The first step in your financial plan is to price your product or service offering. This can be a tough decision as several factors can influence price ... including what your target customer can and is willing to pay, how much your competitors are charging for similar or like services or products, and the quality of your product/service. Beware of setting prices too low at first, because it will be harder to raise the prices later, especially with existing customers.

Next, you want to calculate the *cost of goods (COGS)*. This includes direct costs required to produce or provide a product/service. Examples include raw materials, parts, and labor.

If you are a service-based company such as a coach or consultant, you may not have any costs in producing a product, but you should consider the costs directly associated with delivering the service when pricing your services. Examples of costs to consider are the sales commission or salary you want to pay yourself, any costs required to perform the service such as fees to book a conference room for the meeting, and credit card processing fees. While you may not be able to technically deduct these as COGS on the P&L (you will need to confirm with a CPA), these are costs that affect your bottom line. Also, assuming you want to keep a portion of the sales to reinvest into the company, make sure you also factor that into your financial plan.

Once you have your price and COGS, you can determine *gross profit* — how much the company will net for each product or service that you offer. To calculate gross profit, subtract the COGS from the Sales Price.

Gross Profit = Sales Price – Cost of Goods Sold

If the profit margin is too low or even negative, you will want to adjust the sales price and/or decrease the cost to produce the product or service. If you make no changes, you may have to sell more products or work with more clients than you want or can manage, or risk going into debt. (More details on how adjusting sales price or costs influences how much you need to sell is covered in Chapter 20: Become More Confident in Business Decisions).

Let's assume you are a marketing coach with a home-based business. You want to make a yearly salary of $100,000, take two weeks of vacation as unpaid time, and work an average of 40 hours per week. (I'm not sure any entrepreneur only works 40 hours a week, but let's keep the math simple.) This comes to $50 as a hourly wage. This doesn't account for taxes yet, which you should also consider as your learn more about the impact of taxes on your small business in later chapters.

If you charge $100 per coaching session, have a credit card processing fee of approximately $3 for each coaching session, pay $25 for a conference room for clients who want to meet in-person, then you will have $22 remaining for every coaching session booked. How did I calculate this? $100 per hour coaching session - $50 in wages - $3 credit card processing fee - $25 conference room = $22.

The next two variables that influence your business finances are *operating expenses* and *sales volume*. Operating expenses are costs that are not tied directly to product or service, and are necessary to operate the business, such as selling, administrative, and general *overhead costs*. You will want to calculate and forecast operating expenses on a monthly basis based on sales volume. (More details for operating expenses can be found in Chapter 18: Plan for Every Dollar Earned).

Now that you know your sales price, cost of goods sold, and operating expenses, you have all the key variables need to create one of the most important financial statements for your business called the *Profit and Loss Statement (P&L)*. A P&L is also known as your Income Statement. (More details on creating and finalizing the P&L are described in Chapter 19: Use the Past to Understand What to Change.)

Direct Sellers

For those in direct sales, it is still worthwhile to do a financial plan to understand your costs and predicted income. I've worked with direct sales clients who realized after gathering and analyzing their numbers that they were spending more in operating expenses, such as marketing and meals and entertainment, than they were making in sales.

Commonly asked questions if you are thinking there may be exceptions to needing to create a financial plan.

1. **What if I don't plan to apply for a business loan?**

   It is still advisable to create a financial plan that shows your different products and services offered, pricing, overhead costs, and direct costs. You may find that it is costing too much to produce a particular product or provide a service.

2. **I've been in business for several years and I don't have a business and financial plan. Isn't it too late to do it now?**

   It's never too late. Businesses and the competitive landscape are always evolving, so go ahead and start your business and financial plan now. A financial plan should be continually re-evaluated. If you want to launch a new product, it can help you determine when it will generate a profit. You may find that you are currently offering products that you might retire as they aren't generating the profits that you expected or they aren't exactly in your line of expertise and may be costing you more time to produce or deliver than it is worth.

3. **I'm excited about my idea and want to get started. Can't I just do this later?**

   Invest the time to plan this upfront before you launch your business. Once you start, things get so busy that you will likely find yourself wearing multiple hats in the company and working more hours in your business than you had expected. Then, once you are in the thick of the details, it's a real challenge to take a step back and make those strategic business and financial decisions, if things are not going as expected.

4. **I'm not really good with numbers. How do I even know where to begin?**

   Seek help from a financial coach or find help via reaching and seeking out local resources, such as the Service Corp for Retired Executives

(SCORE). Have someone evaluate your numbers to make sure that your business idea is profitable. If the expenses are too high and your pricing is too low, you may be sinking your business before it even starts.

5. **Can't I just sell more products if my financials aren't doing as well as expected?**

   Sometimes selling more products can actually cost you more money. You have to evaluate all the numbers to understand your *fixed costs* (i.e., rent, advertising, and telephone that stay the same regardless of production output), *variable costs* (i.e., cost of goods sold that vary based on the production volume), and *projected sales* to make sure you are making money. If your variable costs are too high, you may be losing money for every product that you make! (More details on how fixed costs affect your profits in Chapter 20: Become More Confident in Business Decisions).

CASE STUDIES

Here are real-life examples of business owners who didn't fully evaluate product pricing and costs:

Pricing Confusion with Prospective Customers

Laura D., one of my small business clients, prides herself on providing better quality products than her competitors. However, she doesn't charge a premium price for her products, which caused some confusion within the marketplace. One of Laura's clients told her that because her prices were lower than her competitors, it made prospective customers wonder if the quality of her work might be sub-par. After receiving that feedback, she arbitrarily raised the price of all her products by $10. This isn't the best plan to change prices because Laura didn't look at costs per product and have a clear understanding of what the profit margins are, by increasing all products by the same amount. Perhaps one product should actually have been raised by $15 in order to make a profit because the variable costs are higher. If she created a financial plan, she would be more confident in the long-term pricing structure and likely suspected this in advance.

Spending Time on Low Margin Projects

Lexie C., CEO of a landscaping company, was frustrated with the lack of income in her business. After reviewing her product offerings and pricing, we found that she was spending too much time on offering one of the products ... that wasn't even in her line of expertise. It was also costing her money in credit card interest fees due to prepaying of inventory and lag time in invoice payment from customers. After looking at the low profit margin for these types of projects, she decided to remove them from her offering so she could focus on the high profit margin projects.

No Return on Investment with Vendor Booths

Bethany K., a direct seller of a health supplement company, spent $400 on a vendor booth to market her business at a local yoga event. She spent eight hours at the event and had four people who signed up to receive more information about a health class, yet did not sell any products or meet any qualified and interested prospects for joining her company. After a second vendor booth event two weeks later yielded similar results, she realized for her business, that a vendor booth was a high cost with little return. If she had done competitive research to understand marketing costs, projected her expected number of marketing events per month, and typical expected return, she may have realized sooner that she needed to adjust her marketing plan to exclude investing in vendor booths.

The Bottom Line

While many business owners excel in creating the product and providing the service offerings, they are often not great at the financial aspects required to operate a profitable and sustainable business. If you are just starting your business or if you're an existing owner needing the business to bring in more money, take the time to predict the financial success of your company. If you need a loan or investor funding, a well-written business plan with financial data supported by thorough research is even more important and will increase your likelihood of getting your loan approved. Not only will it give those potential backers the confidence that you'll be successful, it will boost your confidence as well. If you are stuck and need help with creating the financial plan, hire a coach who specializes in business and finances to help validate your information and numbers.

Use the template provided at the end of this chapter to calculate the gross margin on all your products and service offerings.

For links to resources and ready-to-use templates referenced in this chapter, visit www.smallbusinessfinancebook.com/kit and enter your email address to gain instant access.

Template: Calculate Gross Profit

Product / Service	Sales Price	Cost of Goods Sold (COGS)	Gross Profit (Sales Price – COGS)

Chapter 3
Avoid that "Oh S*&@!" Moment

Do you cringe when you look at the stacks of papers piled up in your office? Have you ever had your computer crash after having worked on an important file for hours and found yourself staring at a blue screen? It is amazing how quickly papers and key business files pile-up without proper filing, especially if you haven't set up a *document storage system*. This may sound unimportant and something you can put off until you have more time, but having a pile of disorganized paperwork can cost you time and money when you need to search and produce a specific business receipt for a tax audit, or reference a file for an upcoming business meeting. By having the right system for your business in place and regularly saving files on a designated Administrative Day each week, you can avoid that "Oh S*&@!" moment when an unforeseen computer accident occurs, erasing all the files stored on your desktop ... and all you see now is a solid, blue screen. (More on Administrative Day in the next chapter.)

Are you currently saving all your files directly onto your desktop? If so, consider having a server-grade backup solution or a backup to the *cloud.* **Avoid the costly mistake of storing all your critical business files — such as signed contracts — on your desktop, without a backup.** If your laptop is stolen or your computer crashes, you will lose all your important company and client data, and not have a recoverable duplicate. Imagine the wasted hours, stress, and increased costs when you are forced to re-create or track down an immeasurable number of files. This can also put your clients' data at risk, potentially affecting your professional credibility.

Given the accessibility and cost of secure, cloud-based servers, a *virtual storage system* is the best way to guard against data loss. You invest in security, ease of document control, and the ability to access your files anywhere you go, all for a relatively low cost.

Several companies offer options for cloud document storage for as low as five dollars per month or charged based on use. Examples include Microsoft

OneDrive for Business; Box, Inc.; Dropbox Business; and Google Apps for Work – Drive. If you'd rather go with a company that offers free storage, make sure to research the security features of those companies. It is also important to check their terms and conditions, or you may be giving up the intellectual rights to your content unknowingly. You will likely discover that there is a monthly or annual investment or fee to retain content ownership and get the level of security and storage quantity you need. Also, stay up to date on the latest news for any security breaches on the companies that you are considering.

You may want to consider other features such as document and spreadsheet software, collaboration tools, and email when choosing your cloud system so that your entire business operates on the same cloud server.

Tip - Did You Know that if you store your business files in a personal cloud storage system instead of a business (i.e., Dropbox vs. Dropbox Business), that you could lose ownership over your intellectual property? Check the terms and conditions carefully and remember that nothing is free!

In order to be 100% confident of your intellectual property rights, consult an intellectual property attorney to review the binding contractual agreements to which you are agreeing, prior to selecting your cloud solution.

For those who prefer paper storage, use a physical filing system. It can, however, be a mistake to not also have digital storage for your documents. There are risks of fire or theft of the only copy of your important files. Consider also the potential issue of storage space capacity, since you should keep tax-related files for seven to ten years in case of a tax audit. You also need to ensure that you have a scanner that yields a high resolution output ... it has to be legible. Having a cloud-based system allows you to access to your documents whenever or wherever you are. If you are traveling for business and you forget to bring an important file or need to reprint materials for your meeting, you can easily retrieve a digital copy.

If your business requires you to keep all original physical records and you find that space is an issue, there are companies like Iron Mountain or The File Depot that will deliver storage cartons to your location for your records. When you are ready, they will pick up the cartons and store your files in a secure facility with alarm systems, fire detection, and security monitoring.

CASE STUDIES

If you are not yet convinced on how important having a virtual cloud system for your business, I want to share two real-life stories where all files were completely erased and we had that "Oh S*&@!" moment.

A hacker wiped out and erased all the files on computer.

John H., a business colleague who provides IT solutions, shared that one of his clients inadvertently allowed a hacker access to his computer. The hacker installed a virus that wiped out his client's entire desktop! Because this client was saving all his files on his desktop, he lost everything, including his client data! If he had used a secure, cloud-based storage system, the client would have been able to retrieve a copy of his data.

I accidentally overwrote and erased two hours of work.

This is extremely embarrassing to admit, especially given my IT professional background, yet I once made the same mistake that I'm advising you to not make in this chapter! We live and we learn.

I had written and finished this chapter you are reading right now, and saved it on my desktop with my intent being to upload it to my cloud-based server when I got home. It was very late when I finally arrived home, so I decided to wait until the next day. The next morning when I went to review the completed chapter and upload it to the cloud, I realized that I had accidentally saved a different chapter 'over' (on top of) this completed chapter!

Since I had written and saved everything on my desktop, my IT help desk confirmed that it was completely lost in the 'ether.' He advised that had I written the draft within my Office 365 account in Word Online, then a previously saved version would be available from the documented history. What a huge mistake and very fitting that the one and only file that I have lost in over ten years is the very chapter on the importance of creating a document storage system! The one silver lining is proof that we live and we learn ... and I can personally demonstrate the importance of having a digital storage system!

that you know the importance of creating both physical and virtual-,ed storage systems, here are steps on how to implement each:

I. **Physical**

1. Purchase the following items
   - File Cabinet
   - Hanging Folders – 5-tab, assorted colors, letter size
   - File Folders – 3-tab, assorted colors, letter size
   - Label Maker
2. Create and label the hanging folder categories that make sense for your business.

   Example:
   - Red – Finances
   - Orange – Business Admin & Planning
   - Yellow – Legal & IRS
   - Green – Clients & Prospects
   - Blue – Presentations and Handouts
3. Create and label file folders.

   Example of folders in the Finances section
   - Receipts – 2016 Dues & Subscriptions
   - Receipts – 2016 Marketing
   - Receipts – 2016 Meals & Entertainment
   - Receipts – 2016 Office Supplies
   - Receipts – 2016 Training & Development
   - …

By creating a folder for each business deduction type, you easily navigate to the appropriate folder to find a particular receipt if your CPA has a question about it.

The folders should closely match the business expenses types in preparing for tax deductions. This will be covered in more detail in a later chapter. Consult with a CPA to confirm which expenses you can deduct for your specific business.

4. Put the file folders that you created in Step 3 into the related file categories that you created in Step 2. Save your current an receipts and files in the appropriate folder.
5. At the end of the year, create new folders for the next year. If you are running out of physical space, consider alternative storage solutions for files from previous years.

   Remember, if you have too much paper and don't want to store over seven years worth of receipts and paperwork in your office, consider storing previous years in a secured and disaster-resistant storage facility for a monthly or yearly fee.

II. **Virtual**

1. Research three cloud-based systems and determine which will best fit your business needs and budget. Sign up for a free trial (most companies offer this) to test out solution before you commit to a monthly or annual subscription.
2. Create virtual main folders that make sense for your business.

   Example:

   a. 01 - Finances
   b. 02 - Business Admin & Planning
   c. 03 - Legal & IRS
   d. 04 - Clients & Prospects
   e. 05 - Presentations and Handouts

	*Tip – By numbering the folders, you can control the order in which they display. Otherwise, they will display in alphabetical order.*

3. Create virtual sub-folders that make sense for your business.

   Example of folders in the 01 - Finances folder

   - Receipts – 2016 Dues & Subscriptions
   - Receipts – 2016 Marketing
   - Receipts – 2016 Meals & Entertainment

- Receipts – 2016 Office Supplies
- Receipts – 2016 Training & Development
- …

	*Tip: By creating a folder for each business deduction type, you can easily navigate to the appropriate folder to answer any questions that come up.*

The folders should closely match the business expenses types for tax deductions. This will be covered in more detail in a later chapter. Consult with a CPA to confirm which expenses you can deduct for your specific business.

4. Save current and future receipts and files into the appropriate folders and sub-folders you created in Step 2 and Step 3.

   If you decide not to retain physical receipts and paper version of documents (i.e., signed contracts), scan, store the digital files in the appropriate online folder, and shred the originals.

5. At the end of the year, create new folders for the upcoming year.

CASE STUDIES

Here are real-life examples of business owners who couldn't find that one critical business file and who uses email to store important files and receipts.

Can't Find That Presentation File Anywhere?!?

Jessica S., owner of a leadership training company, was paid by a vendor to travel outside of her city and state to teach a training class. She was already stressed because she had spent hours searching for the presentation file that she needed to deliver the training. We met the day before she had to travel and she still hadn't found the file. The result of not finding the file is that Jessica would have to cancel the training and forfeit the money. And, by canceling with short notice, she could potentially affect her reputation as a small business owner.

When I advised Jessica to use a cloud-based system and showed her different options, she realized that she already had a Microsoft OneDrive Business account. In spite of paying fifteen dollars a month for over a year, she had never used the account!

Saving Emailed Receipts

Warren A., a financial advisor, shared that he uses his email provider as a source for all his receipts. He creates a folder for each year, then as he receives receipts, he will move emailed receipts into this folder. He also scans and emails hardcopy receipts to himself, then places them into the appropriate folder.

This all sounds great, of course, once things are under control. However, what if you're so far behind and have such a mess that there are *months* of paperwork to scan and file for recordkeeping? If you have too much paper and want to outsource the work, there are companies like Iron Mountain and The File Depot that will take your paperwork, scan it, and either shred or mail you back the originals, for a monthly subscription or cost per page. You could also hire a personal assistant to get you on-track and let them spend the time prepping and saving the files directly into your preferred document storage system. You will have all your files saved in one place that only you control, as opposed to stored on another company's server. In most cases, the benefits of outsourcing this manual work far outweigh the costs. (If you don't feel that you are making enough money to hire assistance, this will be covered Chapter 15: Know When You Can Afford to Hire Help.)

If you don't have the time or energy to get yourself 'out of the weeds' and have decided it makes sense to outsource, here are steps designed to save you time and minimize stress.

1. Research three personal assistants or local scanning/storage companies that will come to your office to help with gathering, organizing, scanning, and filing the paperwork. Hire the one that you feel will work best for you and your business needs.
2. Purchase the office equipment as recommended above. Some personal assistants may offer errand services so you can also have them

purchase the file cabinet and office equipment, or you can order the items online.

3. Have the assistant file the paperwork in your physical file system and/or cloud-based storage.
4. Have the assistant shred documents as appropriate, or hire a shredding company to come pick up your papers to shred off-site.

The Bottom Line

Protecting your information and intellectual capital is extremely important and easy to do once you have both a physical and a virtual cloud-based storage system in place. Then, remind yourself to save files regularly to prevent any loss of time and work, should your computer fail or succumbs to a virus. Creating the system and managing the process on a regular basis on your designated Administrative Day will be key to avoiding that "Oh S*&@!" moment.

Template: Evaluate Cloud-Based Systems

Cloud-Based Options			
Name of Company			
Plan Type			
Storage Limit			
Monthly Cost			
Free Trial Period			
Additional Features			

Decision Made:

	Monthly Rate	Date Started	Renewal Date
Started Subscription with:_______	_______	_______	_______

Chapter 4
Don't Drown in Receipts

Many small business owners tend to operate *on the fly*. They are so excited to start marketing their business that they haven't taken the time to think through the back office processes. One area that holds small business owners back is managing business receipts. Deciding upfront how to manage business receipts may not be fun, yet it is important to set up a good system and process before things get too busy. Many toss receipts into a shoebox and think that they will get to it later when they have time, but before they know it – they have "the shoebox problem." That is, a box full of jumbled receipts that never stops filling up. Just looking at a sizable mess makes most procrastinate until it becomes critical, typically right before tax time. Without organized business receipts and immediate access to critical paperwork during tax preparation, filing can be stressful, costly, and time-consuming.

When you claim business expenses for tax deductions, the IRS has five to seven years to audit your business. There is no statute of limitations if you are caught guilty of fraud, so the IRS can go back as many years as they want in those situations. If the IRS performs an audit, you either produce the required documentation or you forfeit the deduction if you can't find the receipt. If you have incorrect or no documentation, the IRS would calculate penalties and interest on the amount that was due at the time of the tax return.

Even if you have set up a document storage system as instructed in Chapter 3: Avoid that "Oh S*&@!" Moment, you may still find yourself with "the shoebox problem." The real problem is believing that you will organize your receipts in your downtime. In reality, as a small business owner, there is rarely a 'down time,' so you are most often faced with sorting through them just before tax time. If, however, you wait until quarterly or annual tax season, you may be surprised to find that some of your receipts are hard to read or that there's nothing printed on them at all! The ink on receipts printed on thermal paper will fade within a few weeks! By waiting several months or more to go through your receipts, you may find yourself losing out on tax deductions because you won't be able to claim illegible or blank receipts.

Tip: Did you know...that the ink on receipts printed on thermal paper will fade within weeks? Get those receipts copied or scanned now!

Administrative Day

By scheduling one day once a week, every two weeks, or at least once a month as an administrative day, you can catch up and do all the back office tasks, like managing your receipts. Block out time on your calendar, to avoid getting so busy with meetings that you literally run out of time, or forget to do it and have to push it off to the following week. When scheduling, treat the hours designated that day for administrative tasks the same way you would a client meeting. It is just that important to your business.

If you dread the idea of doing all the administrative work yourself, then hiring part-time help to scan receipts may make more sense. Then you have someone dedicated to making sure this is done on a timely basis. Refer to Chapter 15: Know When You Can Afford to Hire Help for more information on delegating and hiring others to do administrative and ancillary tasks.

One category of business expenses that is highly scrutinized by the IRS is *meals and entertainment*. If they find any issues with your recordkeeping in that category, the next areas of high scrutiny are mileage, advertising, and office supplies.

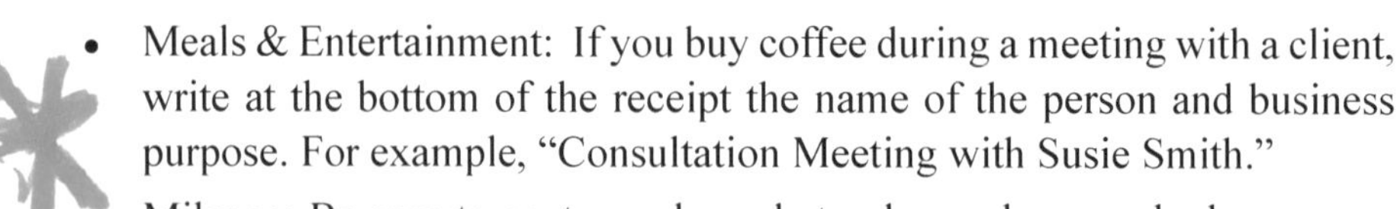

- Meals & Entertainment: If you buy coffee during a meeting with a client, write at the bottom of the receipt the name of the person and business purpose. For example, "Consultation Meeting with Susie Smith."
- Mileage: Be sure to capture who, what, when, where, and why you are claiming this mileage as a business expense. You want to be 100% confident that you have enough information that will hold up in an IRS audit.

Refer to Chapter 10: Make Your Drive Worth It for more information on how to track mileage.

Tip: Check with your CPA for the maximum allowed deduction for your meals and entertainment. Generally, you only get to deduct 50% of meals and entertainment for business, unless the meals were during business travel.

Changing how you organize your receipts allows you to work better with your bookkeeper and CPA. Here are the steps that work well with clients.

1. Decide which day of the week or month will be your administrative day.
2. Block out time on your calendar to go through receipts. Plan on an hour if you have a lot of receipts; perhaps two hours if you choose to go monthly instead of weekly or bi-weekly.
3. When you purchase an item for business, immediately mark at the bottom of the receipt the who and the reason (the why) for the business expense.
    - For example, if you had a coffee meeting with a prospective client, you would write at the bottom "Consultation with <Insert Name of the prospect>."
4. Store the receipt in a temporary location, to be handled during your designated administrative day.
5. On that day, photocopy, scan, or take a picture of each receipt and file/store it in the location you set up in Chapter 3: Avoid that "Oh S*&@!" Moment.
    - Physical Receipts – If you want to keep a physical copy of all the receipts, then you need to photocopy the receipt, staple the original to the photocopy, and then file.
    - Digital Receipts – If you only want to keep a digital copy of the receipts, you need to scan or take a picture of the receipt, file the digital copy, and shred the original physical copy.

	*Tip: Did you know...that the IRS is now more accepting of digital copies for receipts as long as you can easily retrieve and print a legible, unaltered copy upon request?*

CASE STUDY

Here is a real-life example of why you have to avoid "the shoebox problem."

The Danger of Handing Over Bankers Box of Receipts to CPA

David B., a CPA at a large accounting firm, shared with me that you should never hand over a banker's box of receipts to your CPA for tax preparation. You should calculate the total amount spent per business expense type and give that summary information to your CPA in the form of a Profit and Loss Statement (P&L). If the thought of a P&L scares you, no need to worry. Instructions for how to create one using a simple step-by-step process is in Chapter 19: Use the Past to Understand What to Change.

If you provide a handwritten note with all the totals and a banker's box of receipts, depending on the company's policy, your CPA may choose to manually add up all your receipts because you physically handed them all over. He or she may consider it grossly negligent at that point to take your word and not check it, especially if he or she has all the supporting evidence in hand. Given that most CPAs charge anywhere from $125 - $400 per hour, you are looking at a very costly mistake of several hundreds of dollars if you hand over a box of receipts for tax preparation.

	*Tip: Did you know...that if you physically hand over a box of receipts to a CPA, he or she may decide to manually count up all the receipts and not take your word for any totals given? It depends on your CPA's policy and interpretation of the Statement on Standards for Tax Services No. 3 - AICPA.*

If this process seems effective moving forward, yet you need help with the huge stacks of receipts that have piled up for months or even years, there are companies and services that transform receipts into digital files for you. Do the research for the minimum pricing per project and make sure you are comfortable with the security and terms and conditions when you choose your vendor. Companies to consider researching include Iron Mountain, The File Depot, and Shoeboxed. By signing up for a monthly subscription with Shoeboxed, as example, you can send receipts in a pre-paid envelope with a unique code to identify your account. They then scan your receipts and shred or return the originals to you. If you are hesitant to mail your receipts, you can look to hire a private courier, get a tracking number, or directly drop off receipts if you are located near the company. Then, once you are caught up on receipts, you can choose to stop this service and manage receipts on your Administrative Day, so they never pile up again.

Pitfalls of not creating a sustainable process for saving receipts.

- Feeling overwhelmed and behind.
- Finding receipts missing, unreadable, or in a folder or stack that is disorganized.
- Struggling at tax time to find and enter business expenses into your *recordkeeping system.*
- Missing tax *deductions*.
- Incurring tax penalties and interest for insufficient documentation if audited.

The Bottom Line

One of the top pain points that many small business owners share is their desire to be better organized for tax preparation, yet they either don't know how, or don't have the time. By being organized, you can save more money on CPA fees, decrease your anxiety about tax season, feel more confident in your numbers, and eliminate the scrambling to find receipts at the last minute. Avoid losing out on tax deductions because you were too busy running the business and there wasn't enough time to go through all your receipts.

Should you find that you are so far behind that this task will take hours or days to implement, outsource this administrative work to a company or personal assistant who can help to go through and organize your receipts. You will find that the benefits far outweigh the costs. If you're not yet convinced, you'll discover how to be confident and know when you can afford to hire someone to help in Chapter 15: Know When You Can Afford to Hire Help.

Action Items

1. Document in writing your current system and process for managing receipts. Identify any changes you want to make.
2. Design and document your new system and process for managing receipts. Use the template provided at end of chapter.
3. If you determine that you need additional help because there are too many receipts to handle efficiently yourself, research three companies or personal assistants that can help you with current receipts to find the one that best fits your budget and needs.
4. Hire a person or company to get current receipts photocopied or scanned into a file storage system.
5. Weekly/Monthly - Follow the system and process on your designated Administrative Day.

Template: System and Process for Filing Receipts

What is your current system and process for keeping receipts? ____________

____

____

Day of the week: ______________________ or As needed

Time Block: ____________________________ or As-needed

How Often (circle one): Weekly Monthly Quarterly Yearly Never

Storage (circle): Shoebox Filing Cabinet Desktop/Laptop Cloud

# of Receipts that Need to be Copied and Stored: ____________ or Too many to count

Need to outsource and get help to photocopy/scan/store files: Yes No

If need to hire, research: __________ _________ ______________

Decided to hire: ____

New System and Process for Filing Receipts

Day of the week (circle one): Mon Tue Wed Thur Fri Sat Sun

Time Block: ____________________________

How Often (circle one): Once a week Twice a month Once a month

Storage (circle): Filing Cabinet Desktop/Laptop + Back-up Drive Cloud

Additional comments: ____

____

Chapter 5

Select the Right Tax Expert

Understanding what constitutes a deductible business expense can be extremely confusing. You may not realize that something can be claimed as a business expense, and toss away those receipts. By the time you find out, either by engaging with a CPA or through a financially-savvy colleague, it is too late to claim those tax deductions. If you decide to do your own taxes to save the $500 or more in CPA fees, you most often err on the side of caution, and do not deduct expenses that may raise a red flag. Estimating taxes and quarterly payments are another area that can be confusing, which can lead to not paying or saving enough. This is how not knowing what you don't know, can end up negatively impacting your bottom line.

CASE STUDY

Scared to Claim Business Expenses

Harry A., CEO of a video gaming company, shared with me that his wife decided to prepare their taxes after their CPA kept increasing his fees year after year. When discussing his financial questions and challenges, Harry said that his wife was scared to deduct the $200 per month professional club membership that they were paying for his business because she felt it could raise a red flag with the IRS. This membership was costing them $2,400 a year and they were not taking any deductions. On the other hand, they could consult with a CPA for about $150 - $400 per hour to get a definite answer. If it is later found to be a legitimate business expense, the benefits of being able to deduct such expenses each year far outweigh the one-time consultation fee.

Not All CPAs Are Equal

It is worth the investment to hire a CPA for at least for a one hour consultation to answer your questions and validate any assumptions that you have regarding business deductions and tax rates. To prepare for that meeting, make sure you have a list of all your questions and send it ahead of the meeting so the CPA can be prepared. (See the template at the end of the chapter to get you started.)

When selecting a CPA, make sure you do your research and interview at least three before deciding on one. This is a person with whom you will build a relationship as they get to know your business and advise you on tax strategies. Many people will stick with a CPA who is not a good fit because they feel it would take too much time and money to switch to another. Spending time upfront to interview three CPAs pays off when you find one that you like and trust to do the job.

Some CPAs are great at the numbers, but may not give you tax strategies to help you proactively decrease your tax liability. Others are good at both the numbers and advising their clients on tax strategies. Ideally, you want one that can do both well. Be sure to have an active dialog with your CPA throughout the year, especially if there are major changes in your personal and business lives that could affect your taxes.

CASE STUDIES

Is My CPA Too Conservative?

Karen C., a business attorney, told me that several friends and a family member, who is a CPA, said that her current CPA is not aggressive enough. What does that mean? She said that her CPA wouldn't allow her to deduct the home phone line and the cell phone, expenses that she didn't have before she started her business (home phone line) and were increased due to the business (upgraded cell phone plan for additional minutes and data). In this case, it's time to consider interviewing a different CPA.

Some CPAs will offer a complimentary consultation for prospective clients so write down your list of questions or concerns and interview another CPA.

My CPA Doesn't Tell Me Anything

Warren J., CEO of a personal training company, shared that he is unaware of what business expenses he can deduct for the business, and he has been in business for over five years. He said that his CPA doesn't tell him anything. He wants to find another CPA , yet feels like he's too busy right now to launch a search.

While your CPA should be advising you on deductions, you can be proactive and check out the IRS Schedule C (Form 1040) to see the expense categories listed in Part II as a starting point to ask questions.

The easiest and quickest way to learn what expenditures qualif
ness deductions, is to look at the IRS Form - **Schedule C (F**
for Profit or Loss From Business, to determine what categories are lis
and which your company falls into. Also, for general rules for deducting business expenses and specific expenses, refer to the **IRS Publication 535: Business Expenses**. Keep in mind that you should still consult with your CPA even if you have this list, because every business and situation is different and what may be an ordinary and necessary business expense for one company, may not be for another.

Examples of business deductions listed in the IRS Schedule C (Form 1040) are: advertising, legal and professional services, office expenses, rent or lease, repairs and maintenance, supplies, meal and entertainment, and travel.

There is a separate section on the IRS Schedule C (Form 104) for **Other Expenses**. It can be confusing and hard to find information on what business deductions can be listed in this general category. One more great reason to consult a CPA to confirm what is considered an ordinary and necessary expense in your field of business. Examples of other expenses that your bookkeeper or accounting software may track include: Internet, Cell Phone, Bank Service Charges, Dues & Subscriptions, Annual Renewable Computer Software, Shipping & Delivery, and Continuing Education.

Tip: To get more information about business expenses, search the IRS.gov website under Publication 535, Business Expenses. The publication provides a list of common business expenses and explains what is and is not deductible.

Home-Based Businesses

Do you work primarily at home? If so, do you claim business use of your home or do you fear that raises a red flag with the IRS? I've talked to many small business owners who are fearful of an IRS audit so choose not to claim home office expenses. It is always best to consult with a tax professional to discuss your specific situation to understand if you meet the qualifications for claiming home office expenses.

According to the IRS.gov website, several criteria must be met to qualify for deducting expenses for business use of your home, including 1) *exclusively* and regularly using it as your principal place of business, and 2) *exclusively* and regularly as a place where you meet or deal with patients, clients, or customers in the normal course of your trade or business. The key word here is "exclusive." **See IRS Publication 587, Business Use of Your Home** for a list of all the qualifications that must be met, examples, and exclusions.

Self-Employment Tax

Generally, self-employed individuals must pay self-employment tax (SE tax) in addition to income tax. This is a Social Security and Medicare tax. Check with your CPA to determine if you are subject to self-employment tax and income tax.

The Bottom Line

You started your business to focus on what you enjoyed doing – creating products or providing a service that you love, and you aren't a tax expert. Avoid doing your own taxes to feel confident that you didn't overpay or underpay. The instructions on tax forms can be confusing and you can waste time and lose sleep trying to understand them. There are many rules that seem to change, making it well worth the money to pay a CPA who keeps up with new IRS changes and requirements, and enables you to maximize your tax deductions.

Action Items

1. Take the time to interview three CPAs. Referrals from trusted business colleagues are recommended. Use the template provided at the end of this chapter to write down names and notes about the CPAs.
2. Review the list of expenses on the Schedule C Form.
3. Create a list of questions regarding potential business deductions. Use the template provided at the end of the chapter to structure your meeting with each CPA.
4. Book a consultation meeting with the CPAs you want to interview and make a decision to hire the one you trust and that provides what you need.

Template: Research for CPAs (if you don't already have one you like):

	CPA	Referred By	Scheduled Consultation Date	Rate Per Hour
1				
2				
3				

Decision Made:

Date Hired:

CPA selected: ____________________ ____________________

Template: CPA Consultation Meeting

CPA Interviewed: ____________________

Date Interviewed: ____________________

1. What is my estimated tax rate? ____________________
2. What types of expenses are considered ordinary and necessary for my business?
3. Do I qualify to deduct home office expenses?
4. Should I be tracking business mileage and/or actual vehicle costs and repairs?
5. Do you offer monthly rates for tax advice throughout the entire year?
6. ____
7. ____
8. ____
9. ____
10. ____

Tip: Take copies of your tax returns for the last two years when meeting with a CPA. To give you a definite answer on your tax rate, the CPA will need to review them.

Chapter 6
Make Tax Day Less Stressful

Understanding how taxes can work for your businesses is often challenging, even for the best of us. Most business owners get stressed simply by thinking about *them*. Most fear and anxiety comes from business owners not fully understanding the impact of taxes ... until they calculate and pay the tax bill for the first time. The financial "bite" taxes can take out of your profit can be shocking. If you don't save appropriately and don't have enough cash to pay your estimated quarterly taxes or annual tax bill, you may end up owing the government and paying interest until you can pay off the balance. Once you get into this cycle of debt, it can be very difficult to get out. Some business owners will decide to buckle down and work harder to make more sales to pay off the debt. Others give up and close up shop. It is unfortunate that many business owners decide owning a business isn't worth the effort to get out of this cycle, because small businesses are such an essential part of our economy. The potential stress and surprise can be avoided by consistently working with a CPA, understanding your tax rate, and creating a system to save aside enough money to make the payment(s).

The Biggest Disconnect about Taxes

If you used to work for a company, your employer paid your federal and state taxes. When you received your paycheck, those taxes were already taken out on your behalf, so no action was needed on your part. Now, when you have your own business and make a sale, the client pays you and you receive the full amount at the time of the sale. No one has taken taxes out yet. This is where many small business owners make their mistake. Since there is not a standard guideline or requirement for how this money gets set-aside (because the government only looks at receiving its money), many small business owners spend all of that money (before taxes), not realizing the cost of not saving for taxes ... until, that is, they get their first big tax bill!

A Typical Scenario

Small business owners make a sale and the money is deposited directly into the business checking account. This practice continues for all sales made throughout the month and year, i.e,. money is directly deposited and sits in the checking account. When making business decisions on business purchases, they take a draw or distribution, or pay for training and development, using the current checking account balance as the deciding factor if they can *afford* it.

(If you don't have a business checking account, refer back to Chapter 1: Separate Personal and Business Expenses. If you want to learn more about draw or distribution, refer to Chapter 7: Pay Day the Right Way.)

Now, fast-forward to tax time. These same business owners now learn they owe several thousand dollars for taxes, but there is no money in the checking account to cover that bill. Many small business owners are stuck at this point because they didn't realize how much money they would owe and have already overspent. Now they owe taxes and will be charged interest until they can pay off the balance.

Tip: Paying an accountant to calculate and pay all of your quarterly taxes is an additional expense, but may be worth the peace of mind.

CASE STUDIES:

Here are two real-life stories about the consequences of not paying taxes:

Don't Skip a Quarterly Payment

Victoria B., a former gift shop owner in New Jersey, shared that she received a significant penalty for not filing her quarterly taxes due for opening her shop for just one weekend. She had made several sales over the weekend, then left for France for three months. She made the assumption that because she didn't really owe much or any taxes for opening her shop for only three days that quarter, that she could just skip that quarterly estimated payment. She was unaware that she was required to provide information every quarter. When she was audited eight months later, she was given a fine of $100 per month for each month that she didn't pay tax, as well as an interest penalty. She realizes now that she should have taken the few minutes to send in paperwork, but instead received an $800 tax penalty lesson.

Several months later, she was audited again and was given a second penalty for not paying taxes. She had learned from her previous mistake and was certain that she had paid. After going through all her records and receipts, she found that she had accidentally paid her taxes twice so the state actually owed her money! When she informed them of her mistake and asked for her money back, she got no response. Five years later, she still hasn't gotten her money back.

Business Mistakes Caused Strain in Family Relationship

Allison K. shared with me that she goes out of her way to document everything correctly for her personal training business, after her father unintentionally mismanaged his medical supply company. Among other missteps, her father mixed personal and business expenses, causing numerous tax and legal headaches that put a strain on Allison's family. At one point, Allison worried that her father's mistakes might cause him to be led away in handcuffs.

Tip: Business owners have to pay estimated quarterly taxes when they have a tax liability of $1,000 or more based on combined personal and business tax liability. Check with a tax professional to see if you should be saving 100% of last year's tax liability or 90% of this year's estimated tax liability in order to pay enough estimated taxes to avoid any underpayment penalties.

By implementing the following steps, you can make tax day less stressful and be sure to have enough cash for taxes.

1. Consult with a CPA to understand the tax implications for your business. Refer back to Chapter 5: Select the Right Tax Expert if you don't have a CPA.

Tip: The best time to engage with a CPA is ***before*** *you start your business. Have them estimate your tax rate and provide tax considerations based on the products, services and promotions that you plan to offer customers. Keep in mind that tax brackets are progressive, so the more you make, the more you owe.*

If you have already started your business, be sure to engage with the CPA throughout the year, especially if there are any major changes.

2. Confirm your tax rate to calculate how much to save in your business savings account for estimated tax payments. Be sure to also account for self-employment tax of 15.3% (as of the writing of this book) on net profits if you have a sole proprietorship, LLC (that has not elected S-Corp).

Tip: If you don't know your tax rate, a good number to start saving is between 25% - 30% until you can confirm with a CPA. Your tax rate is made up of the federal tax (minimum is 10%), state tax (varies), and self-employment tax (15.3% if applicable).

3. Mark your calendar with federal and state quarterly tax payment due dates. Be sure to mail your payment to arrive on time. Generally, if you mail your payment and it postmarked on or before the due date, the IRS will consider it to be on time.

Payment Period	**Due Date**
January 1 – March 31	April 15
April 1 – May 31	June 15
June 1 – August 31	September 15
September 1 – December 31	January 15 of following year

Based on IRS.gov website, if the due date for making an estimated tax payment falls on a Saturday, Sunday, or legal holiday, the payment will be on time if you make it on the next day that is not a Saturday, Sunday, or legal holiday.

4. Calculate the taxes owed based on net profits and save this amount in your business savings account. Do this process on a monthly basis so you don't run the risk of spending money that isn't yours to spend. When calculating the amount of taxes you owe, there are two options.

Option 1: The Hand-Off Approach

To make sure you save enough for taxes and avoid penalties for underpaying estimated taxes, you can take what the IRS calls the *safe harbor* method and pay at least 100% of your prior year's tax liability (or 110% if your adjusted gross income is over $150,000) over the four quarterly due dates. To make it more confusing, the percentage changes to 90% if you expect this year's sales to be greater than last year. Consult with a tax professional to make sure you are using the correct percentage in calculating your taxes owed.

While the safe harbor approach ensures you don't get penalized for any underpayment by making the estimated quarterly payments, it doesn't mean that you have paid all you owe. If at the end of the tax year your actual tax liability is higher than what was estimated through the safe harbor approach, you will need to also pay the difference when you file taxes. Make sure you build a cash cushion and still have money on hand if you choose this approach.

For example, let's see how the safe harbor approach works in the following scenarios.

Scenario 1: If you owed $20,000 in taxes last year, then assuming your income is *less* than $150,000, you would make estimated tax payments of $20,000 this year. Your estimated quarterly payments come out to $20,000 divided by 4 = $5,000 per quarter.

Scenario 2: If you owed $20,000 in taxes last year, but your income is *over* $150,000, then for this year, you would make estimated tax payments of $22,000 because $20,000 x 1.1% = $22,000. Your estimated quarterly payments are $22,000 divided by 4 = $5,500 per quarter.

Scenario 3: If you calculated that your estimated tax payment of $22,000 by the safe harbor method, but your actual tax liability is $25,000, then you will have to come up with another $3,000 when you file your taxes.

Option 2: Hands-On Approach

Calculating your taxes after preparing your monthly Profit and Loss Statement (P&L) is more accurate, and a more hands-on approach to calculating the taxes you owe. Wait until you close the books on the last day of the month, create the P&L, and calculate taxes owed based on your tax rate. Be sure to be consistent and mark it on your calendar as a recurring task so you don't forget to do this!

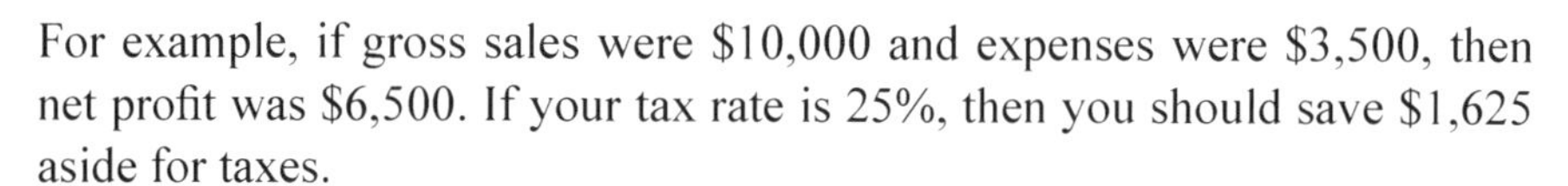

For example, if gross sales were $10,000 and expenses were $3,500, then net profit was $6,500. If your tax rate is 25%, then you should save $1,625 aside for taxes.

$$\$10{,}000 - \$3{,}500 = \$6{,}500$$

$$\$6{,}500 \times 0.25 = \$1{,}625$$

NOTE: If you don't know how to create a Profit & Loss Statement, refer to Chapter 19: Use the Past to Understand What to Change.

5. Transfer the calculated tax amount ($1,625 example in Option 2 above) into your business tax savings account. If you don't have a bank account dedicated for tax savings, refer back to Chapter 1: Separate Personal and Business Expenses.

	*Tip: Set-up a recurring task on your calendar to calculate taxes owed and transfer that amount from your business checking to your business savings account for taxes. Doing this on a consistent basis will ensure that you never run out of money for taxes!*

6. When taxes come due, use the money in your business savings account. Keep track of the estimated payment made and the exact date that it was made. Your CPA will need to know the amount and dates in the event of an audit.

	*Tip: By setting aside money each month for taxes based on the tax rate calculated by your CPA, you will never run out of money to pay your taxes again!*

7. When meeting with your CPA to prepare taxes, organize your paperwork and information in the following order.
   a. Equity / Loans
   b. Business Expenses / Deductions
   c. Profit and Loss Statement

In addition to the taxes on your income, there are other taxes to consider. Sales and use taxes can cause issues when small business owners don't understand how their business activities affect taxes owed. *Sales tax* is imposed on retail transactions for tangible items sold. *Use tax* is also imposed on retail transactions, and is applied when the merchant buys a product, then converts for his or her own use without having paid tax on the initial purchase. These two taxes are mutually exclusive, so either a sales tax or use tax applies to each single transaction.

CASE STUDY

Here is a real-life story about the consequences of not engaging a CPA earlier.

I Have To Pay A What?

Laura B., an independent consultant for a women's clothing line, said that in the early stages of her business, she gave away free products to generate interest and increase her mailing list. She purchased products at wholesale for her inventory, yet failed to ring them up as sales in her invoicing system because she was giving the products away for free. However, by not recording those transactions anywhere, sales tax was neither collected nor paid. When she met with her CPA to prepare her taxes for her first year in business, Laura received some bad news. She owed taxes on all the products that she had given away for free, because the government requires someone to pay the taxes. She was obviously upset and wished someone had advised her to keep track of these free giveaways and promotions, and that she needed to pay a use tax on them!

The Bottom Line

Do yourself and your business a favor and hire a CPA for at least a one hour consultation, especially if you are struggling to understand your tax liability. Average hourly CPA rate can range anywhere from $150 - $400 per hour, which is well worth the advice to ensure you are doing things correctly and avoiding penalties for underpayment of taxes or not paying taxes at all. Don't assume that your spouse, who does your personal taxes via tax software, should handle your small business finances. While CPAs are experts on taxes, they almost always have someone else review their work. When you or your spouse do your own taxes, there are no *checks and balances*. Instead, hire a professional to make tax day less stressful.

<table>
<tr>
<td></td>
<td>Tip: Did you know...that CPAs are required to take continuing professional education (CPE) hours to maintain a CPA license? In many states, this requirement is an average of 40 CPE hours a year.</td>
</tr>
</table>

Chapter 7
Pay Day the Right Way

Finding the best way to pay yourself can be challenging. Paying yourself is also called a *draw* or *distribution*, depending on your legal entity. When you first started your business, you were probably so busy getting your first sale that you may not have thought through how much money you need to bring into the business. You know you need money, and you may be afraid to pay yourself. A draw or distribution may be hard to do when the business is just starting or when you experience a slow month for sales. Then, when you need to pay your personal bills, you may make the mistake of commingling your business and personal finances if you don't have a clear, repeatable plan for how to pay yourself. Another common scenario is that you wait until you have paid all your business expenses to see how much you can pay yourself, and could be disappointed when there is little left for personal needs. To correctly calculate and set up pay day in a logical, productive way, you will also need to factor in an emergency cushion, the amount of cash you want to always have in your business account to cover the fixed costs in the event of unexpected slow months or emergencies.

How do you currently pay yourself? Choose from the list below.

A. I don't. My business is not making enough money yet.

B. I withdraw money from the ATM whenever I need it.

C. I use my business credit card to pay for personal expenses when I see there is enough money.

D. Both B and C.

E. I write myself a check from the business account and deposit it into my personal checking account. (Or I do an online transfer between accounts.)

The correct answer is E.

There are three ways to pay yourself: 1) write yourself a check 2) set up an online draft from the business checking account, and 3) set yourself as a payee via online banking and have the business send you payments.

Be sure to add details in the check memo area to indicate it was your pay. When you do that, there is a clean paper or digital trail showing that money was taken out of the business in the form of a draw or distribution. If you are ever audited or your CPA wants to re-calculate your numbers, you can easily review the bank statements with cleared checks and refer to memos in online drafts for verification.

Let's take a look at what the potential consequences are if you are currently doing any combination of A, B, or C.

A. **I Don't Pay Myself.** While it is usually expected that as you grow the business you may not be drawing money from the business, at some point there has to be income. If not, what's the point of being in business? Would you go to work for a company that never paid you?

Tip: Did you know... if the business isn't making any money after a certain number of years, the IRS may consider what you are doing a hobby, and you may lose your ability to claim as a business?

B. **I Withdraw Money from the ATM.** Withdrawing money from the ATM in various amounts whenever you have a personal financial emergency, will open you up to an administrative nightmare if and when you have to go through an audit and explain why you made each withdrawal. Avoid this practice to save yourself time and stress.

C. **I Use My Business Debit/Credit Card for Personal Expenses.** Avoid commingling funds. **This is worth repeating ... avoid commingling funds.** If you accidentally claim a draw or distribution as a business expense and the IRS catches it in an audit, you will be penalized for underpaying taxes.

If you have already been commingling your business and personal finances, no need to panic. You can start to make changes now by going back through all those personal transactions that you paid for with your business card and mark them as a draw or distribution. It can be a difficult task, yet doing it now prevents a later regret.

Once you have cleaned up your books, remember that the business debit and credit card should only be used for business expenses. If you need the business to pay you, then write yourself a check in the form of a pay day.

CASE STUDY

Here's a real-life story from a client who was afraid to pay herself.

Caroline D., a small business owner who also had a part-time job, could make thousands of dollars in sales one month, but then only a few hundred dollars the next. Since business sales fluctuated so drastically, she was afraid to pay herself a set amount on a consistent schedule. Instead, she would just look at the balance of her business checking account to see if there was money. If there was, when purchasing personal items for her family, she would use her business credit card as a "pay day" method of the business paying her. Big mistake! By using her business credit card to pay for personal items, she has now commingled funds, which will lead to an accounting and audit nightmare.

Let's pretend that she gets caught incorrectly claiming $1,000 of expenses as business office supplies that were actually personal expenses for the 2016 tax year. She will be penalized for underpayment of taxes, and the interest is calculated from the date that she would have owed taxes.

In other words, she should have paid taxes on the $1,000 by April 15, 2017 and not been allowed to deduct that from her income. If the IRS catches it in 2020, the interest starts accruing as of April 15, 2017, even though the IRS didn't audit her until 2020.

When I advised creating a set amount to pay herself each month, she got nervous and said that she didn't want to pay herself when the business was slow. I asked her, "Would you be upset if a company you worked for decided not to pay you one month because they were afraid that business was a little slow that month?" It is not always easy for us to think about it from that perspective, yet you have to treat your own small business like a corporation, and yourself as an employee. Not knowing when or how much to expect in pay each month would make any employee upset and ready to quit. Ask yourself and be honest, "Would I want to work for myself?"

Consider these two options to make sure you pay yourself. Decide which option is best for you and then follow the steps to set up your pay day to minimize administrative paperwork and potential IRS issues. Use the template provided at the end of the chapter to document your decisions.

1. Determine how much you need to have as an emergency cash cushion. This is the number that will cover fixed costs in the event of emergencies or help cover unexpected slow months. (The importance of having a cash cushion is discussed in more detail in Chapter 17: Build a Cash Cushion for Greater Flexibility.)

Tip: If creating a budget seems daunting or if you are in debt, contact a financial coach to review your current income and liabilities to help you create a working budget and make recommendations for debt elimination.

Option 1: Set Amount. If you aren't sure what amount to select, then first step is to create a personal budget and determine what you need in income to pay your personal bills, or at least to break-even each month.

Note: If creating a budget seems daunting or if you are in debt, contact a financial coach to review your current income and liabilities to help you create a working budget and make recommendations for debt elimination.

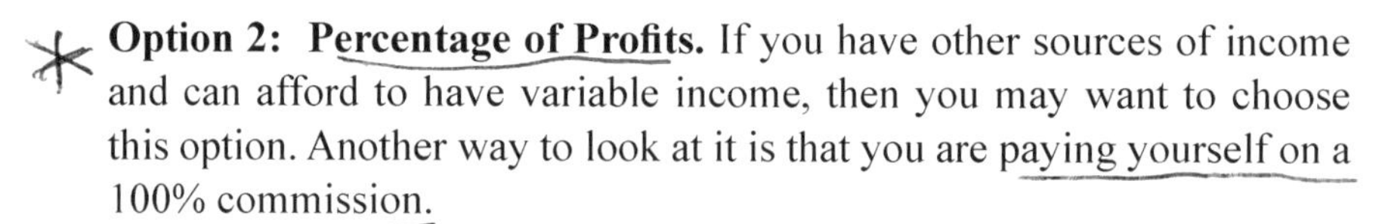

Option 2: Percentage of Profits. If you have other sources of income and can afford to have variable income, then you may want to choose this option. Another way to look at it is that you are paying yourself on a 100% commission.

Tip: Picking a set amount to pay yourself is the easier method in terms of time commitment, but you need to be sure that your business generates enough income that can support your paycheck. For the months that your business does better than expected, put that money aside in your business savings account to cover those slow months.

2. Decide when and how often you want to be paid.

   Option 1: If you want a set amount each month, pick a date(s) of the month to designate as pay day(s). Be consistent and make your pay days sacred; don't vary on the dates from month-to-month. I prefer once a month pay days, on the same date every month. The more often you pay yourself (such as twice a month), the more administrative work you put on yourself by having to write a pay day check and keep track of date and amount of the draw or distribution.

	*Tip: I like pay days on the 21st of the month. Since many of us have big bills like a personal mortgage due on the 1st of the month, picking a pay day like the 21st of the month gives you plenty of time for the business to write a paycheck, deposit the check into your personal checking account, and set up payment to arrive on time for those personal bills due on the 1st of the month.*

To make this even more efficient, you can set up automatic draft payments for both your paychecks and personal bill payments each month.

Option 2: If you want a percentage of each month's net profits, then you pay yourself once a month based on a pre-determined percentage of each month's profits. You can only pay yourself after you reach month-end and calculate your total sales, cost of goods sold, total expenses, and net profit. These numbers are used to create a Profit and Loss Statement (P&L), an important statement that your CPA needs to do your taxes that will be discussed further in Chapter 19: Use the Past to Understand What to Change. You will also need to calculate the amount of taxes that you owe and need to save into your business savings account prior to paying yourself, to make sure there is enough money to pay yourself the percentage that you've selected.

When selecting your designated pay day, you can give yourself a couple of days to finish closing the previous month's numbers and calculate your "commission amount."

	*Tip: For this method, I prefer pay days on the 7th of the month. This allows you time to close the prior month's books, calculate your draw or distribution amount, and write yourself a check.*

3. Pay yourself the right way.

	*Tip: Get the business to pay for itself, before you pay yourself. You have to make sure your monthly expenses are addressed.*

Option 1: If you selected a set amount each month, then automate your paychecks. Set up an automatic bank account rule in your business checking account to either send a check or transfer money into your personal checking account on the date that you determined is your pay day.

Option 2: If you selected paycheck as a percentage of each month's net profits, here are the steps you take each month:

1. At month-end, create your Profit & Loss Statement and calculate how much the business made that month after cost of goods sold and expenses, otherwise known as net profits.
2. Take the amount left in net profits and subtract the money that should be left in the account for an emergency fund and/or next month's bills. (More on why you need an emergency fund is in Chapter 17: Build a Cash Cushion for Greater Flexibility.)
3. Take the percentage that you determined as your "commission" and multiply that by the amount left in Step 2. The number you just calculated is your pay day amount.
4. Write yourself a check from the business based on the amount calculated in Step 3.

	*Tip: Even if you don't have consistent monthly net profits, you can still start your recurring pay days by picking Option 2. You will pay yourself a pre-determined percentage on each month's net profit.*

CASE STUDY

Here is an example of Eager Elaine, owner of Fantastic Products, LLC, who had a great month in sales, with $7,000 in profits after paying all the monthly obligations and bills. She always wants to keep $3,000 in her business checking account as a "cash cushion" and reserve in the event of emergencies. She has a tax rate of 25% and wants to take home $2,000 each month.

Question: Can she afford to pay herself $2,000 and if so, how much does she have left to put aside for future reinvestments into the company?

P&L Month Close	$7,000
Emergency Cushion Baseline	$3,000
Tax Rate	25%
Amount to put into Business Savings Account for Taxes	$1,750
Paycheck	$2,000
Amount to put into Business Savings Accounts	$250

Answer: Yes, she can afford to pay herself $2,000 that month and will have $250 that she can reinvest for future needs.

To see how this was calculated:

Amount to Save for Taxes = $7,000 x 25% = $1,750

Amount left to Save for Retained Earnings and Future Investment = ($7,000 - $3,000 - $1,750 - $2,000) = $250

Tip: Did you know...that if you are self-employed and your business is registered as a sole proprietorship or LLC, your taxable income is on what the business made, not on what you paid yourself?

The Bottom Line

Learning how to correctly pay yourself first is an important step in keeping clean accounting books and staying in business. If you have made the mistake of using business funds for personal use, it is time to stop and correct this practice now. Be sure to go back through and flag any expenses that should be considered a draw or distribution. Having separate business and personal bank accounts, and knowing your personal budget numbers, can make you more successful both in correctly paying yourself and paying yourself enough money to support your lifestyle.

Template: Setting Up Draw or Distribution

Option 1: Set Amount

Income Needed per Month: ____________________

of "Paychecks" per Month ____________________

Emergency Cushion: ____________________

Amount per "Paycheck:" ____________________

Pay Day: ____________________ of the month

Option 2: % of Profits

Month	
P&L Month Close	
Emergency Cushion Baseline	
Tax Rate	
Amount Put into Savings Account for Taxes	
Paycheck	
Amount Put into Savings Accounts for Retained Earning/Future Investments	

Part II:

Construct Strong Walls & Infrastructure

"Each of us is carving a stone, erecting a column,
or cutting a piece of stained glass
in the construction of something much bigger
than ourselves."
— Adrienne Clarkson

Chapter 8

Collect Money to Stay in Business

To stay *in* business, you need to collect money from your customers. You may be so busy trying to make the sale, that you don't fully understand and haven't evaluated your options for invoicing and payment systems. Such an important decision warrants investing time to find the right systems for your business. Some owners will go with the one that they hear about most or choose one based on the lowest fees. Later they find the system may be more complicated than expected or not robust enough for what they need. When you choose an invoicing and payment system that fits your business and financial needs, it affects your bottom line by making it easy for clients to pay you.

Direct Sales

If you are in direct sales, most likely your company provides the invoicing and payment solution that you need to use. However, direct sales consultants have told me that on occasion, they will have issues with the company's tool. Then at the last minute, they will sign up and rely on another payment solution to finalize a sale. In those cases, you should read on to understand what factors to consider.

7 Key factors to consider when comparing invoicing and payment solutions

1. Do they offer a device to swipe and take payment in-person? If so, what does the device cost?
2. What are the fees for swiping a credit card?
3. What are the fees if the credit card information is manually entered rather than swiped? (This is usually a higher rate.)
4. What is the fee for invoices created and emailed?
5. Will you be able to process payments directly on your website?

6. How long does it take for funds to become available in your account?
7. Will you need to set up recurring or subscription payments (e.g., charge clients on a monthly basis or on some other set schedule)?

Several commonly used, well-known companies that provide invoicing and payment solutions include PayPal, Square, Freshbooks, Xero, and QuickBooks. I used Square when I first started my business and I really liked it because of the easy-to-use interface. I recently switched, however, to Freshbooks, which provides invoicing, payment processing, and accounting all in one tool. QuickBooks also provides similar features as Freshbooks. If you are considering merchant accounts offered by your banks, keep in mind that with the fees, bank merchant services are usually better for larger businesses with a significant number of transactions.

If you sell a subscription-based service or decide to offer long-term payment plans, then you want to pick a payment system that allows for recurring invoices or that can store and automatically bill to your clients' credit card. Otherwise, you will have to go in on a monthly basis and figure out *who* you have to bill and *when*. Manual processes may work at the beginning of your business, but it is time-consuming and not sustainable as your business grows.

Once you have researched and picked an invoicing and payment solution, you can start creating and sending your invoices. You will want to add your logo, list of products or services, hourly rate, costs, and any terms and conditions. Send out a test invoice to make sure you're happy with the look-and-feel and user experience. You will find that the address that is on your profile when you created your account is displayed automatically on your invoices, so please make sure this isn't your home address! Having a business address and email address will protect your privacy, as well as make your company appear more professional.

Tip: The address that you provide when setting up your profile with an invoicing and payment system is automatically displayed on invoices. Renting a P.O. Box, which can be as low as $70 a year, is a cost-effective way to have a business address and protect the privacy of your home address.

Some services may still require you to use a physical address and do not allow for a P.O. Box. In those cases, look for those post office locations that allow the use of their street address for your P.O. Box. Another option is to research companies like Regus and Executive Office Suites that provide shared office spaces and offer business address services. Then, you can list their business address on your business cards, website, and general mailing. They collect all your packages and mail, and can forward your mail to a specified location.

CASE STUDY

Real-life example of a small business owner who had no invoicing system.

I know a contractor who used to write his invoice on a sheet of paper that he ripped out of a spiral notebook, with a handwritten list of tasks completed, cost of materials, and a final total. It was really unprofessional and made me question if one of us was getting ripped off. He has since moved to an invoicing system that shows time spent on the job versus detailed list of materials purchased.

Let's take a look at an example of two business owners who swipe vs. manually enter in credit card information, and see how the fees charged and money deposited are different.

1. **Swiping Sam** takes a credit card payment for $1,000. He has no problem with his PayPal credit card reader, so he swipes the credit card and completes the transaction.
2. **Manual Matt** also takes a credit card payment for $1,000. However, his PayPal reader isn't working so he manually keys in the customer's credit card information.

	Swiping Sam	Manual Matt
Sales Amount	$1,000	$1,000
Swipe vs. Manually Enter Fees	2.7%	3.5% + $0.15
Fees	$27.00	$35.15
Deposited Amount	$973.00	$964.85
Difference	$8.15	

Due to a broken credit card reader, Manual Matt earned $8.15 less than Swiping Sam for the same sales amount. That may not seem like a large amount, but imagine what would happen if Manual Matt went the entire day, week, or several weeks without getting this resolved. Ten transactions a day at $1,000 per sale over ten business days would cost Manual Matt $815! Over time and with thousands of transactions, this can add up to be a significant number and drastically cut his profits. Typically, the fees are higher to discourage merchants from manually entering in numbers and increasing the chance of human error.

CASE STUDY

Real-life example of a small business owner not making it as easy for clients to pay.

Elizabeth L., a seasoned business owner who charges clients on average $2,000 per project, told me that she doesn't accept credit card payments anymore because she panicked after her first big sale and saw how much was taken out for credit card payment fees. She is now only accepting checks. She could make it as easy as possible for clients to pay by credit card simply by factoring processing fees into her pricing.

Now that you know all the factors to consider when selecting the best invoicing and payment system for your business, do you have a consistent process for how you will handle it when a customer signs-up or purchases a monthly subscription package in the middle of a billing cycle? For example, when would you bill a customer who signs up on the 20th of the month for a three month subscription? Selecting an invoicing system like Freshbooks or QuickBooks allows you to create recurring profiles with start date, frequency, and duration. You can save yourself time and billing headaches by automating the process rather than having to remember to send out and chase down payments.

The Bottom Line

When evaluating and choosing your invoicing and payment solution, be sure to look at factors from your business that will impact your decision. If you are having a difficult time deciding which system to use, take advantage of the free trials that most offer before committing to a monthly subscription.

Also, remember to take into account the fees when creating your pri
for your products and services. Credit card processing fees are a cost of doing business, and making sure that you are still making a profit based on your sales price and fees is part of running a business. Keep track of the service charges and credit card processing fees to confirm with your CPA that these are deductible business expenses.

Tip: Take advantage of free trials before committing to a monthly subscription when selecting your invoicing and payment system. If your free trial is about to expire and you didn't have enough time to evaluate and make a decision, contact the company. Sometimes, they will extend the free trial.

Use the template provided to evaluate invoicing and payment options.

For links to resources and ready-to-use templates referenced in this chapter, visit www.smallbusinessfinancebook.com/kit and enter your email address to gain instant access.

Template: Evaluate Invoicing & Payment Solutions

Company	Freshbooks	Square	
Device? (Y/N)			
Swipe Rate*			
Emailed Invoice Rate*			
Manually Entered Rate*			
# Days until Funds Available			

*Note: Fees are generally higher with American Express than Visa / MasterCard.

Chapter 9

Don't Go Broke Over Monthly and Yearly Obligations

Most of you started your own businesses because you wanted the freedom and independence to do what you loved. Many of you, however, likely hate the numbers. While you may not like numbers or feel competent working with them, this can be a make it or break it area for your business. Creating a realistic budget is critical to your success and allows you to understand if you are spending more money on your business than you expected, and if you are slowly going broke over items like dues and subscriptions and other monthly commitments (software tools and business development).

Many small business owners do not accurately budget for membership dues or tools with monthly and yearly subscriptions to support their businesses. Even if you don't intend to grow your business quickly, you may not plan for rapid success, but it happens. Then you are left scrambling, trying to find tools, hire help, or invest in training to quickly get up to speed and catch up.

Before I started my business, I had done research and used estimates in my business and financial plan. Six months into my business, I realized that I didn't have a complete understanding of what it would take to run the business more efficiently and what networking groups were going to be the best for me to attend to find prospects or meet referral partners. It wasn't until I met like-minded small business owners and mentors who provided great recommendations did I fully appreciate which tools and networking groups were the ones to use and grow my business.

Software Subscriptions

Signing up for several $10 - $15 per month tools to support or run your business can initially seem like no big deal. Some fees are higher and start at over $25 per month, such as SurveyMonkey, which allows you to poll people attending a specific event and customize surveys with your logo.

Then, every once in awhile, you sign up for something that requires a year-long commitment to get the lower rate. Before you know it, you have signed up for multiple subscriptions and committed yourself to monthly and yearly obligations that can quickly add up to several hundred dollars. Unless you keep a detailed calendar of when you sign-up for a subscription, you may forget about it until you get an automatic billing notice and renewal. You may even end up investing in something that you don't even use anymore! (If annual subscriptions tend to sneak up on you, feel free to jump to Chapter 14: Never Be Surprised About Incoming Bills Again.)

Perhaps signing up for multiple subscriptions and owing too much in monthly and yearly subscriptions is not your main issue. You may be the type of business owner who tries to do everything that requires no investment as much as possible and doesn't sign up for many subscriptions. Although it's great that you are mindful of what you spend, be careful of any terms and conditions when doing things at no cost. Also, investing nothing on business tools can limit the growth of your company if you are spending more time doing tedious, manual or administrative work, rather than working on your business. Periodically evaluate how you're spending your time when working in your business and determine if there are things that you are doing that can be done more quickly by investing in a monthly subscription.

Monthly Website Expense - Stock Photos

Assume nothing is free. If there is no monetary cost, check the attribution requirements. For free photos, you often have to clearly attribute the source, which is what I found with sites like Flickr. Other sites like Pixabay state that you can use their images, even for commercial use, all without giving credit to the artist, but it also says that depicted content may still be protected by trademarks, publicity, or privacy rights. That seems too confusing for me, so I stay away from sites like those because I don't want to have to spend time searching for the specific rules for each photo that I may want to use.

One site that I really like for images is Death to the Stock Photo (DTS). It clearly states that you can use the photos without attribution. I even emailed the help desk to re-confirm this, because I wanted to be 100% certain that I could use the photos for my blog posts without the risk of someone trying to sue me. I received an email back within twenty-four hours, confirming that yes, the photos could be used without attribution or link back to the site. I actually loved the photos from DTS so much that I upgraded to their premium package to gain access to more photos, for only $15 per month. A year later, I realized that I hadn't used any images for the last six months, so canceled my subscription. While $15 per month doesn't seem like a lot, that adds up to $180 per year, which then totals to $900 over five years, $1,800 over ten years, and so on. You get the point.

Always do a yearly audit of your expenses to make sure you are actually using what you are purchasing. Ideally, review it quarterly and create a recurring task on your calendar.

There are also sites like StockUnlimited that will provide access to thousands of stock photos for a set fee. For example, at the time of writing this book, StockUnlimited is offering a package of $89 for lifetime access to 600,000 vectors and photos. It is worth spending the extra money to be absolutely certain that the images you use and post on your website are safe to use.

If you are just starting your business and not sure if you want to make a big monetary commitment, another site that I really like is photodune.net, which sells royalty free stock photos from $1 - $7 per image, with the price based on image size.

Even if you do pay for an image, it may available only for informational use. In those cases, you won't be able to use it for commercial use, such as on printed material that you plan to sell. If uncertain, you can always contact the company and ask. It's better to be safe than sorry.

CASE STUDY

Using Images Without Permission

Alex J., owner of a financial coaching business, had an unfortunate experience of receiving a cease and desist letter for a stock photo that was posted on his company's website. One of the developers on his team had uploaded the photo without checking the license and permissions of use for that photo. To avoid a lawsuit for unauthorized use, Alex took the conservative route and just shut down his website because he could not be 100% certain of the other thousands of images that his team had posted. Since stock photos can cost as low a few cents (if purchasing in bulk or as monthly subscription) to $1 per photo, he decided to start his website over from scratch and replace every single image before re-publishing. It took Alex over three years to re-launch his website after having to search and replace all the images.

Membership Dues

It's easy to begin joining several networking groups and find yourself investing more money than you had anticipated. Are you clear about your goals when joining a membership group? Do you compare the cost of joining against the value and the anticipated return on investment? Most networking groups will allow you to participate in a free trial period before they ask you to commit.

Tip: Treat joining networking groups like dating. Go on a couple of dates to make sure it's the right fit before you commit!

In addition to the dues for networking groups, make sure you also account for the meals, entertainment, and travel associated with attendance. Many groups have networking luncheons with speakers and costs can range anywhere from $15 - $40 per luncheon, so be sure to plan for the luncheons and fees when deciding to join a networking group.

If you find that you are spending a lot of money on membership dues and don't believe you've gotten enough value, it is time to re-evaluate what your goals are and if the right people are at these events. Joe Novara, author of *Intentional Networking*, is a networking coach who advises small business owners to focus on establishing referral and business partners to expand their businesses. It is usually more effective and less expensive to find a partner who does business with the same types of customers that you are targeting, rather than going from networking group to networking group trying to find a prospect.

Finding a group of networking partners all in one place is an effective way to quickly build a referral base. Stephen Hand, BNI Chapter Director of Raleigh, NC, says that joining a local Business Network International (BNI) chapter can grow your network exponentially, by being the only one of your profession allowed in your chapter. With a group of twenty or more professionals who meet weekly, the goal is to know each other's businesses intimately and be able to send each other warm referrals without any direct competition. These referrals are then tracked, and you can see how many referrals were received and who referred the most business to you. According to Stephen, "Ideally every member should be in profit within five weeks. Our average member receives more than $20,000 in the first year." While there are exceptions, Stephen shared how one builder received $35,000 in sales the first year he joined BNI, and has made more than $2 million in profits every year since!

As mentioned earlier, make sure the group is the right fit before you join and check out a couple of local chapters before you commit to a membership. The cost to join can be considered very high for some small business owners and certain professions may not do as well in that environment.

CASE STUDY

Here is a real-life example of what I had estimated for my dues and subscriptions prior to launching my business vs. the reality of what I ended up paying and budgeting for after my first year in business.

Monthly Obligations

Category Type	Company	Monthly Cost
Stock Photos (As Needed)	Various	$10
Membership Dues	Raleigh City Club	$107
Cloud-based Storage	Office 365	$10
Total Monthly Cost (A)		$127

Yearly Obligations

Category Type	Company	Yearly Cost
N/A	N/A	N/A
Total Yearly Cost (B)		$0

In reality, after launching and working on my business - here is what my current and budgeted dues and subscriptions cost:

Monthly Obligations

Category Type	Company	Monthly Cost
Stock Photos Subscription	Death to the Stock Photo	$15
Membership Dues	Raleigh City Club	$0
Cloud-based Storage	Microsoft Office 365	$10
Email Marketing	MailChimp	$10
Scheduling / Calendar	Calendly	$10
Customer Relationship Management (CRM)	Zoho	$25
Mileage App	MilesIQ	$6
Survey (Customized)	SurveyMonkey	$26
Total Monthly Cost (A)		$101

Yearly Obligations

Category Type	Company	Yearly Cost
Website Hosting	InMotion Hosting	$132
Email Domain	GoDaddy	$123
Membership Dues	WBON-Cary	$75
Membership Dues	Vend Raleigh	$35
Membership Dues	AMA	$220
Total Yearly Cost (B)		$585

Total Monthly Cost for Obligations = $101 (A)

Total Yearly Cost for Obligations = $585 (B)

Average Monthly Cost for Obligations = $585 (B) ÷ 12 = $48.75 (C)

Monthly Budget for Obligations: $101 (A) + $48.75 (C) = $149.75 (D)

Yearly Budget for Obligations: ($101 (A) x 12) + $585 (B) = $1,797 (E)

I originally estimated $127 in monthly obligations, yet in reality I need to budget $149.75 per month to cover my monthly and yearly obligations. That's a delta of $48.75 per month, which totals to ***$585 per year that I didn't originally budget for!***

When I also factor in the meals associated with attending the monthly membership events, that increases my monthly expenses by $62. That may not seem like a lot, but $62 per month over 12 months comes out to an additional $744 per year, which totals to $3,720 over five years.

It's easy to see how you can slowly go into debt if you aren't careful and don't budget enough for expenses.

Professional and Membership Associations

When first starting your business, you are likely unaware of all the different professional and membership associations available. Based on my research and recommendations received from seasoned business colleagues, here are some to consider: Chambers of Commerce, Toastmasters International, and National Association of Women Business Owners.

Periodically re-evaluate these networking groups and your return on investment. Even if you love the group and are friends with members, remember you are in the business to make money. If you aren't getting the results you want, it may be time to move on.

The Bottom Line

If you don't know upfront, all the tools you need to run your business, signing up for subscriptions can slowly cause you to go into debt. Accurately forecasting and budgeting will help you avoid running out of money.

Talk with other trusted business colleagues, especially those in similar fields, to gain a better understanding of the tools and networking groups they found valuable. Research for yourself and decide what the total costs are for the ones that you find necessary to support running your business more effectively and efficiently. Usually this number is higher than you originally expected or planned. Having a realistic idea of total costs can impact how you run your business. The numbers affect bigger business decisions such as setting prices and creating marketing promotions. Doing your homework protects your budget and helps make sure you are getting maximum value from your monthly dues, subscriptions, and other obligations.

Use the template provided at the end of the chapter and compile a list of all your dues and subscriptions, and obligation costs. Does the number surprise you? If yes, is it higher than you expected? Evaluate the results from being part of these groups and using the tools, and eliminate the ones that are not working well for you or that you no longer use.

Template: Calculate Monthly & Yearly Obligations

Monthly Obligations

Category Type	Company	Monthly Cost
Total Monthly Cost (A)		

Yearly Obligations

Category Type	Company	Yearly Cost
Total Yearly Cost (B)		

Monthly: Total Monthly Cost $__________________ (A)

Yearly: Total Yearly Cost $ __________________ (B)

Average Monthly Cost: _________________ (B) ÷ 12 = _________ (C)

Need to Budget Per Month: ________ (A) + _____ (C) = ______ (D)

Need to Budget Per Year: (____ (A) x 12) + _____ (B) = _____ (E)

Chapter 10

Make Your Drive Worth It

In any given work week, you drive to meet prospects, work on-site with clients, go to the store to purchase office supplies, and go to the post office to ship packages to customers. In your hurry (or lack of a consistent process), you may forget to track your business mileage. It is easy to forget to start the mileage app on your phone or write down your beginning odometer reading if you are rushing out the door or multi-tasking by taking a call while driving to your next meeting. Even if you do remember, you might forget to stop the mileage app or write down the ending odometer reading. Depending on the type of business and how often you are driving to meet clients and do business errands, the miles can add up to a significant tax deduction! You want to make every mile count and take advantage of this tax-saving opportunity.

There are two options for deducting your vehicle expenses.

Option 1: Standard Mileage Rate

The easier option is to multiply the standard mileage rate by the total number of business miles you drive. You can't deduct actual expenses like oil changes and tire replacements. Mileage reimbursement for 2016 tax year is $0.54 per mile. According to the IRS website, if you want to use standard mileage rate, "you must choose to use it in the first year the car is available for use in your business. Then, in later years, you can choose to use the standard mileage rate or actual expenses." This means, if you chose to deduct actual expenses in your first year of business (Option 2), instead of standard mileage rate (Option 1), you can't switch. The rule holds true even if in later years the standard mileage rate would provide you with a larger deduction.

Option 2: Actual Expenses - Topic 510 - Business Use of Car

The IRS website states that to deduct actual use, you need to keep records of "what it actually costs to operate the car for the portion of the overall use of the car that is business use. Include gas, oil, repairs, tires, insurance, registration fees, licenses, and depreciation (or lease payments) attributable to the portion of the total miles driven that are business miles."

Steps required to track and deduct actual expenses for Option 2

1. Track the beginning and ending vehicle odometer reading for the tax year. Subtract the Beginning-of-Year Odometer reading from End-of-Year Odometer reading to calculate the total number of miles driven:

Total Miles Driven = End-of-Year Odometer – Beginning-of-Year Odometer

2. Add the total number of miles driven for business to find the **Total Business Miles**. NOTE: In order to do that, you must have detailed mileage log of all the business trips and total number of miles per trip.
3. Next, calculate the **percentage of business** use of the vehicle by dividing the Total Business Miles by Total Miles Driven.

$$\textbf{\% of Business Use} = \frac{\text{Total Business Miles}}{\text{Total Miles Driven}}$$

4. Track of all your receipts for expenses related to maintenance and repair of the car. You will be allowed to deduct expenses based on your percentage of business use.

Once you have decided between Option 1 or 2 for tax deductions

1. Pick a method to track your business mileage:
   - **Pen and Paper.** Pick up a mileage log from any office supply store and keep it in your car.
   - **Spreadsheet.** Create a template to capture the necessary information and input your data. NOTE: Refer to the end of the chapter for a template to get you started.
   - **Mileage App.** Use one of the various applications available through your smartphone. Some apps have made it even easier with GPS motion-tracking, which will auto-calculate the starting and ending mileage once your car is moving over a certain speed.

Examples of Mileage Apps to check out that have free and paid versions include – MilesIQ, TripLog, Taxbot, Shoeboxed, and Deductr. Check out terms and conditions to confirm these apps meet the security and privacy that you want.

2. Keep track of key information needed for tax purposes, including:
    - Beginning-of-year odometer reading
    - End-of-year odometer reading
    - For each trip:
        - Date
        - Starting and ending odometer
        - Total number of business miles
        - Business purpose (include details such as name, place, and type of business activity). Refer to template at the end of the chapter for example.
        - Car Driven (important if you drive more than one car for business).

CASE STUDY

Real-life example of a small business owner who paid to recreate a mileage log.

Brianna J. is a realtor who hires a college student once a year to re-create her business mileage log based on her calendar appointments. She knows that she doesn't document everything in her calendar, especially errands related to business vs. actual client meetings. She figures, however, it is better than nothing. She knows that she is missing out on business mileage deductions, but wants to be safe, rather than sorry, if she is ever audited. By not tracking her business mileage as it occurs, she spends approximately $150 per tax season for someone to recreate her mileage log. Is that expense worth it?

She has to drive over 278 miles to just break-even on paying the college student: $150 / $0.54 per mile = 277.7.

Commonly Asked Questions

1. **What if I haven't been tracking all of my mileage. Is it too late to start now?**

    No, it is not too late to start now. The IRS will allow you to re-create your mileage log on a one-time basis; however, to substantiate and support your claim, the log needs to be based on some reference documentation, such as your appointment calendar.

Invest an hour or two to sit down, go through your calendar appointments and business receipts (if you drove somewhere to purchase something), and then re-create a mileage log. It needs to be a written or electronic version with enough details to show the business purpose and total number of business miles. If you are re-creating this, you won't have beginning and ending odometer for each trip; use mapping software like Google Maps or Waze to calculate the total number of miles.

2. **What if I track everything *except* for the starting and ending odometer reading for each trip. Am I screwed?!?**

   No. You are lucky here. The more details that you can provide, the better. Start tracking this now.

3. **What if I want to use actual expenses, but I don't have my beginning and ending odometer reading for the year?**

   See if you can find two repair or car maintenance receipts with odometer readings; one near the first of the year and the other near the end of the year. This can provide the information needed to approximate the beginning-of-year and end-of-year odometer readings.

   Starting now, making sure to maintain a current mileage log so you don't have to go back and estimate the information. You may also want to take a photograph of the beginning-of-year and end-of-year odometer readings with date stamp for proof.

Two examples for small business owners where tracking vs. not tracking business mileage affects tax deductions

Absentminded Abbey forgets to track all her miles and ultimately decides it is too much trouble. She doesn't really drive enough to justify the hassle. From her home-based business she drives to the post office to ship orders at least three times a week. On average, she drives 30 miles a week between her house and the post office. When she attends two networking meeting in one week, she puts 40 more miles on her car. Without realizing it, Abbey is driving an average of 70 miles a week.

Conscientious Cathy wants to claim as many legitimate tax deductions as possible and she always remembers to track everything with her mileage app. Cathy drives about four hundred miles per week. As a buyer's agent showing clients prospective homes, she will typically accumulate 20,000 miles.

	Absentminded Abbey	Conscientious Cathy
Miles per week	70	400
Miles per year (assume 2 week vacation)	3,500	20,000
Standard deduction per mile (2016 is $0.54 per mile)	$0.54	$0.54
Total Mileage Deduction	$1,890	$10,800

The Calculations

Absentminded Abbey

70 miles per week x 50 weeks = 3,500 miles per year x 0.54 per mile = $1,890

Conscientious Cathy

400 miles per week x 50 weeks = 20,000 miles per year x 0.54 per mile = $10,800

The Bottom Line

Remember that anything you do to support your business should be documented; therefore, don't forget your travel (going to the post office, meeting with your CPA, going to training or networking events). While it may not seem like you drive a lot, the miles can and do add up to what can be a significant tax deduction opportunity. Take fifteen minutes to create a documentation process that you will use consistently and you are on the way to making your drive worthwhile.

Action Items

1. Decide which mileage tracking method will work best for you.
2. Create a consistent and daily process to track your starting and ending odometer readings.
3. For tax preparation:
    - If you have chosen to track your mileage via pen and paper or spreadsheet, be sure that you calculate the totals for the year before submitting to your CPA.

- If you have chosen to use a mileage app, be sure to get a report of the total mileage with details and send to your CPA.

For links to resources and ready-to-use templates referenced in this chapter, visit www.smallbusinessfinancebook.com/kit and enter your email address to gain instant access.

Template: Making the Drive Worth It

Do you have a way to track mileage expenses now? (circle one): Yes No

If yes, what process is used?

____

____

____

If the answer is no, why doesn't your current process work?

____

____

____

If your current process isn't working, which option(s) fits best with your lifestyle?

- Pen and paper
- Spreadsheet
- Mileage app

What next steps do you need to take to put this in place?

____

____

____

Template: Mileage Tracker

Here is an example of a mileage tracker to get you started. If you have more than one car that you use for business and personal, be sure to keep track mileage for each car separately.

Date	Starting Odometer	Ending Odometer	Total Business Miles	Address	Business Purpose	Car Driven

Chapter 11

Avoid Late Fees and Insufficient Funds

Late fees and overdraft fees can really eat up your bottom line. **They are a waste of your money!** They can be easily avoided by knowing what you owe each month and creating a process to automatically pay your bills on time. According to an analysis done by SNL Financial and CNNMoney[3], America's three biggest banks – JP Morgan Chase, Bank of America, and Wells Fargo – earned more than $6 billion just from ATM and overdraft fees in 2015. That is a lot of money out of our pockets, and it's easy to see how this happens.

Have you ever forgotten to pay a credit card bill on time, so you got hit with a late fee and interest penalty? Have you ever run out of cash and had to go to the nearest ATM, which wasn't your bank and paid an extra fee to use it? Do you cringe when you realize that you don't have enough money set aside for those fixed expenses and are charged overdraft fees? To solve the late fees and insufficient funds penalty issues, create an automated process to pay bills on time and save money for those annual bills.

Avoid Late Fees with Credit Cards

To manage the credit card bills, many credit card companies offer a feature that allows you to schedule recurring monthly auto-payments so the payment is made on time without your active involvement. You can choose to set up the auto-payments to pay the minimum due, the entire balance, or another amount.

Steps to set up automatic payment from your business checking.

1. Log into credit card account online and look for payment options.

NOTE: If this is your first time logging into the system, you will need to create a login and password.

2. Select the option to manage auto-payment.
3. Select the credit card bill you want to pay.
4. Set up the payment to come from your business checking account.

NOTE: If you don't have a checking account dedicated to the business, refer back to Chapter 1: Separate Personal and Business Expenses.

5. Select a payment date.
6. Select the amount to pay, including options of last statement balance, minimum payment due, total balance, or other amount.
7. Confirm auto-payment and date that it will go into effect.

Tip: Did you know...that you can ruin your business credit score by not paying your credit card bills on time? Set up a process to have this automated so you are never late!

For those who are not comfortable with the credit card companies auto-drafting payments directly from their business checking account, you have two options.

Option 1 : Use Banking Bill Pay

1. Log into your banking account online and select the online bill pay for business checking account.
2. Set up the credit card company as a payee.
3. When you know the payment amount, select the date for the bank to send payment and enter the payment amount. The best is to select a date a few days prior to the actual due date.
4. Mark on your calendar as a reoccurring task the date to review and ensure the bill was paid on time.

Tip: Set up automatic payments for the minimum requirements just in case "life happens" and you forget to make a payment. You can always go back in and make an additional online payment.

Option 2: Write a Check

1. This is the manual option. Just write a check and put it in the mail.
2. Mark the due dates on your calendar as a reoccurring task to review and ensure that payment was received and processed on time. The best is to pay this a few days prior to the actual due date, allowing extra time for delivery.

Tip: Verify that payment has been processed before the due date. Sometimes there can be errors and a payment didn't get received on-time or at all, especially if mailing a physical check. Avoid surprises and nasty letters stating that you have incurred a late fee and services will be terminated!

Avoid Insufficient Funds Fees for Annual Expenses

For annual expenses, you want to save aside money on a monthly basis to have the funds when those bills are due. Since this is money that is already "spent" in terms of financial obligations, avoid letting that money sit in your regular business checking account because it is easy to think that the business has more available cash that it really does. The best way to ensure you have all the money for bills when they are due is to transfer that money into a savings account.

Steps to ensure there are sufficient funds, especially for those larger expenses.

1. Document the average monthly expenses that you need to save for in order to cover recurring annual business expenses, such as website domain renewal, membership dues, insurance, and conference fees.

   NOTE: If you don't know this number, go back to Chapter 9: Don't Go Broke Over Monthly and Yearly Obligations.
2. Create a 'rule' to automatically save and transfer the amount of money calculated in Step 1 from your business checking account into your business savings account.

   Select the frequency and timing for the savings rule, such as once a month on the first day of the month, and enter the amount.

   If you don't have a business savings account, see Chapter 1: Separate Personal and Business Expenses. You may want to coordinate the timing and frequency of this savings rule based on your own pay day that you set up in Chapter 7: Pay Day the Right Way.

3. When you receive an annual billing statement, transfer the money that you had been saving from your savings account to checking account.

   NOTE: If you find that transferring money from one account to another and then back again to pay annual bills requires too many steps, you can always put the money into another checking account that is designated for these larger, annual expenses. Then you can always make payments directly from this second checking account that you are treating as a "savings account" for larger bills.

4. Now you have the funds in your checking account to pay your annual expenses on time.

   Whenever you add new annual obligations to your fixed expenses, like association dues and subscriptions, be sure to re-calculate and update your monthly savings rule.

CASE STUDY

Overdraft fee and interest penalties that totaled over $1,000!

Nathan J., a former owner of a publications company, shared his unfortunate experience. It seems an employee registered the company for a monthly subscription service with an existing vendor, without Nathan's knowledge and approval. The vendor was paid through an automatic draft from the company's business checking account. A month later, Nathan decided to switch banks and closed the business checking account with the original bank.

Several months later, Nathan received a letter from his former bank that he had been charged an overdraft fee due to the vendor submitting for an automatic payment and Nathan having insufficient funds in that account. Despite closing his bank account, he was charged an overdraft fee and interest penalty. As Nathan worked with his CPA to understand how to best resolve the issue, interest penalties accrued to over $1,000 in just six months! Nathan paid off the balance to put the matter behind him. His big lesson learned? Using a business credit card for auto-payments versus automatic bank drafts could have protected him in this particular case.

If his vendor had tried to submit a charge to a credit card that was closed, the vendor would have been notified that the payment was not successful and it was an invalid transaction. Then, the vendor would have likely just contacted the owner and asked for an updated payment information or new payment method, with no penalties incurred.

The Bottom Line

Online banking and technology has come a long way toward making it easy to pay on time. The key is to fully use the technology to your advantage by being sure you set up rules or processes to save for annual bills, ensure there are sufficient funds in the checking accounts, and create automatic payments to avoid late fees and interest penalties.

Template: Take Credit Card Inventory

1. **Have you ever incurred a late fee and interest penalty on any of your credit card bills or other obligations?**

   ____

   ____

2. **If yes, what method would work best for you to automate the bill payment process?**

   ____

   ____

   ____

3. **Take inventory of all your credit cards and set up automatic bill payment:**

Credit Card Company	Due Date	Rule Created: Payment Date	Rule Created: Amount of Payment	Rule Created: Bank Account to Link to Payment

Template: Automate Savings for Annual Expenses

1. Total Expenses Billed Annually: ______________________________
2. Average Monthly Savings Needed: Total Expenses Billed Annually divided by 12: __________________
3. Savings Rule (circle one): weekly twice a month monthly
4. If Weekly, preferred day of the week (circle one): Mon Tues Wed Thurs Fri
5. If Twice a Month, preferred dates of the month: __________ and __________
6. If Monthly, preferred date of the month: _________
7. Checking Account (last four digits): _________________ (to withdraw $ for savings)
8. Savings Account (last four digits): _________________ (to transfer $ into)

Chapter 12
Download Your Bank Statements

Now that banks and credit card companies are encouraging business owners to go paperless, you may already be taking advantage of e-statements. E-statements are a convenient way to review your numbers monthly, and it is important to save them to your computer. Although e-statements are *green* and save physical storage space, most banks and credit card companies provide access to your e-statements for only 12–18 months. Anything beyond that time period is not available online unless you submit a request for access. Not being able to easily access prior years' financial information can have a significant impact on your operating costs when you consider potential bank fees, tax penalties, interest charges, and lack of information needed to make good business decisions. Let's take a closer look at how failure to save statements today can cost you later.

According to the Small Business Audit FAQs on the IRS website, generally the IRS will request the last three years in an audit. If they find substantial errors, they will go back as far as six years. If they suspect fraud, there are no statues of limitations as to how far back they will request. Now that you know that bank and credit card statements are typically only available for 12–18 months, what happens if they are no longer online and you didn't save them? The bank can still access your records, but there may be a delay in getting access to prior years and for some banks, you may have to submit a request to get those printed, and could be charged per statement or by the hour!

Banks vary on their fees for producing statements no longer online. As example, one community bank in North Carolina is charging $5 per statement if you want statements within the last three years. However, if you need the last six years, those additional years are in their archival system which someone will access and print statements for a fee of $30 per hour. Depending on how much bank activity you do, this could mean anywhere from four to fifteen or more pages per statement since the entire statement, including a copy of cleared checks has to be printed. In comparison, a business banker for a national bank shared that their small business clients are charged $5 per statement if they need statements that are no longer online. If you are audited and need two years of statements that are no longer available online, that comes to $5 x 24 months = $120.

What You Need

- ❑ Document Storage System – file cabinet or virtual cloud system (Refer to Chapter 3: Avoid that "Oh S*&@!" Moment for more details.)
- ❑ Scanner (if you want to store physical paper digitally).

Once you have selected your document storage system, if you created a Finance folder as suggested in Chapter 3: Avoid that "Oh S*&@!" Moment, then you can create a sub-folder for Statements. Next, go online to each of your bank account and credit card accounts, download all the statements that are available, and save them into the Statements folder.

Let's take a look at an example of two small business owners to see how these fees can really add up.

Busy Bob was audited by the IRS for the last three years of his business. He didn't save any of his bank statements because he didn't know he had to keep them. He has on average four pages per statement.

Fraudulent Fran was audited by the IRS for some questionable tax deductions. She was audited for the last six years of her business. She didn't save any of her bank statements. She runs a very busy business so has on average fifteen pages per statement. It takes the bank employee approximately ten hours to retrieve and print all the records in the archival system.

	Busy Bob	**Fraudulent Fran**
# of Years Audited	3	6
Number of Statement Needed	36	72
Average Number of Pages per Stmt	4	15
Cost per statement (up to 3 years)	$5	$5
Cost per hour (if archival system)	$30	$30
# of hours charged	0	10
Total Bank Fees	**$180**	**$480**

To see how this was calculated:

Busy Bob

(3 years x 12 months x $5 per monthly statement) + ($30 hourly fee x 0 hours) = $180 fee

Fraudulent Fran

(3 years x 12 months x $5 per monthly statement) + ($30 hourly fee x 10 hours) = $480 fee

Fraudulent Fran spent $300 more in fees because she had to show three additional tax years and she had more bank activity.

Once you get into the habit of saving all your monthly bank statements to avoid unnecessary bank fees, you will also benefit from having this historical data to do monthly and yearly comparisons. This can be done either manually in spreadsheets or via accounting tools like QuickBooks. If and when you decide to hire a bookkeeper and accountant, they can load your previous numbers into their accounting tool. When you can see all the numbers in one place, you make sound business decisions and spot any trends or unusual changes. For example, when Jess McLamb, founder of The Roper Group, was able to easily spot that her business cell phone bill had increased by almost $100 from one month to the next, she was able to quickly investigate and determine why.

In accessing and saving your monthly e-bank statements, you can also keep an eye on your account balances and be more aware of any fraudulent activities sooner than later.

CASE STUDY

A real-life example of a small business owner who was given fake bank statements.

Fake Bank Statements

Dr. Wes, owner of a dental practice, shared with me the importance of knowing what your bank statements look like and checking in on your online bank accounts. He had hired an office manager to keep his accounting and finances in order, and would meet with her once a week to review the paper bank statements and the accounting ledgers of income and expenses for the week.

One day, the IRS showed up, angry that he had been dodging their calls and meetings, and said he owed over $12,000 in back tax payments. Dr. Wes was confused and said he had never gotten any messages or letters from the IRS. He told them that he worked with his office manager on a weekly basis to review the finances and had bank statements to verify that he paid his quarterly taxes.

To his dismay, what Dr. Wes found out was that his office manager had embezzled the money, destroyed the letters from the IRS about the late payments, purposely scheduled IRS meetings when he was out of town, and showed him fake paper bank statements during their meetings.

The Bottom Line

At one point or another, many of us have probably been overcharged for something and didn't realize it until months or even as much as a year later. By having all your financial data in one place, you can easily view what you paid a vendor in the previous month and determine if there are any questionable increases. Even if you aren't ready to deal with your numbers yet, having the historical statements can allow you to use them when you are ready to take a closer look. Then you can make an informed business decision if you need to do things differently.

Take five minutes to download and save your monthly statements in your document storage system. This is an easy win, so start now and make this a recurring task to do on your Administrative Day.

Chapter 13
Collect on Outstanding Invoices

While you don't need to be an accountant to better manage your business, you need to have a good handle on the numbers to maximize your chances of staying in business. One area that can easily get out of control is outstanding (unpaid) invoices from clients. If there are too many invoices that haven't been paid, it can cause cash flow issues. At some point, sooner rather than later for most companies, the lack of cash flow will affect how long the business can pay its own bills. If your business falls behind on payments or runs out of cash, you may be at risk for closing the business because you didn't have a handle on what's outstanding and didn't collect on those invoices. The great news is that there are tools to help you with this common issue.

Automated Tools

There are companies that provide tools (with a monthly or yearly subscription) to help you easily understand what invoices are outstanding. If you create and send invoices through companies like Square, Freshbooks, or QuickBooks, as example, they have summaries and accounts aging reports that will show you the total amount in outstanding invoices owed you (also known as accounts receivable), how long it's been outstanding (also known as accounts aging), and the customer who owes money.

If you are just starting out and are not ready to sign-up for a monthly subscription yet, here is a simple, manual process that you can implement for free.

1. Create a spreadsheet to track the total amount for products and services owed by each customer with start date and due dates. Save this file as "Accounts Receivable – YYYY.MM.DD.xls"
2. Create a task in your calendar for the due dates to follow up if payment has not been received.

3. When payment is received, mark the amount and date received in your spreadsheet and close the invoice.
4. If payment is not received, follow up when prompted by your task reminder.

If you are having issues collecting money owed to you, what are your options to encourage clients to make payments on those outstanding invoices?

1. Send reminder notices for invoices that are outstanding. Tools like FreshBooks have options that allow you click a button to re-send the invoice, and QuickBooks allows you to create customer statements.
2. Add late payment fees to past due invoices. Be sure to check what the maximum penalty is in your state.
3. Create a payment plan for customers with outstanding invoices.
4. Write-off the outstanding amount. While this is not ideal, sometimes you just know that the customer will never pay.

	*Tip: Be sure to research the rules in your state for the maximum late fees and interest rates that you are allowed to charge for past due invoices.*

What could you change to prevent having a lot of outstanding invoices in the future?

1. Change your payment requirements to have customers pay a deposit or 100% upfront, before products and goods are created/delivered or services rendered.
2. Incentivize customers to pay upfront by giving discounts like 5% if paid in full.
3. Make sure it's easy for customers to pay. Review Chapter 8: Collect Money to Stay in Business for payment options if you are currently only accepting cash or checks.

The Bottom Line:

Create an invoicing and payment process that makes it easy for you to track who owes the business, how much, and when it is due. Automated tools are great for providing real-time status based on what invoices were sent, received, and not paid. Keeping informed and having a better handle on your company's financial status allows you to follow up systematically on outstanding invoices. Since you are in the business to make money, create a process to collect on your money, or risk going out business!

Chapter 14

Never Be Surprised About Incoming Bills Again

When you owe money to another business and the payment is not yet due, it should be tracked as a liability, also known as accounts payable. Do you have a good method of tracking these bills? Or are you completely shocked when you get invoices 60 to 90 days later? If you don't have the cash to pay for the bills when they are due, this is typically when you start the cycle of going into debt by putting the charges on your credit card, not paying the balance in full, and incurring interest charges until you pay the debt off. There are better ways, including a simple template included at the end of this chapter, to track these liabilities so that you aren't surprised by these incoming bills and end up owing more money than you have available.

Steps to Stop Feeling Surprised About Incoming Bills

1. For every agreement that you have signed for services or purchases when you aren't billed immediately, or you have to only put down a deposit, track the total amount owed in an Accounts Payable Ledger. NOTE: Refer to the template at the end of this chapter to get started.

   Within the Accounts Payable Ledger, you want to track the following information:

   - Name of the company
   - Total Cost
   - Due date
   - Deposit or 1st payment paid
   - 2nd payment, 3rd payment, etc. made
   - Remaining balance due

2. When reviewing your business financials on a weekly and monthly basis, make sure to take into account the total amount owed in Accounts Payable when looking at the total balance in business checking account.

3. If you find that your Accounts Payable balance is significantly high (i.e., over $1,000), transfer that money into the business savings account to help separate the funds and not be tempted to spend money that is already accounted for.
4. Plan to pay off Accounts Payable as quickly as possible.

It's easy to forget about the money owed, especially when there is a significant lag time between signing an agreement with a company, paying an initial deposit, and having to pay the total remaining balance.

	*Tip: If there are contracts that are over a significant amount (i.e. over $1,000), transfer the money into a business savings account **before** you commit to purchasing the product or service. If you don't have the cash, then you can't afford it!*

CASE STUDY

Real-life Personal Example

In February, I signed an agreement with a design consultant to complete a re-design of my website. I paid the required 50% deposit to move forward, and then waited while she worked on my website. There was, however, a significant delay that put the project three months behind schedule. When the website launched, the contractor sent the final invoice six months after the initial invoice for an amount close to $1,500. If I had not had a good accounting system for tracking this liability, it would have been easy to have already spent this money on other expenses and not be able to settle this large bill.

The Bottom Line

You need to keep a detailed record of all liabilities as they occur, so you always have a handle on how much is owed and when the total is due. Being diligent with tracking your Accounts Payable will help ensure you are never surprised by those large bills again.

Template: Track Accounts Payable

Date	Invoice #	Company	Total Amount	Due Date	Deposit / Payment 1	Payment 2	Balance Due
Example: 3/1/16	50355	ABC	$500	7/1/16	$250		$250

Chapter 15
Know When You Can Afford to Hire Help

As a small business owner, you will wear multiple hats and fill several or all the roles within your business. This is common in early years because owners are just starting out and may not be able to afford to hire someone. So you end up doing tasks that you don't enjoy and maybe are not good at. You also may fill your days doing tasks that don't generate any income for the business, and are what Productivity Coach, Marcey Rader, best-selling author of Beyond Travel – A Road Warrior's Survival Guide, calls "the $10 tasks." How do you know when you can afford to outsource and hire someone to do the tasks that you don't like?

Rader, who has a service helping business owners find and work with virtual assistants, states that small business owners have a short window for hiring an assistant. If they engage too early, they don't have enough money or work to give them. If they wait too long, they don't have time to properly train. It is critical to begin writing down all the tasks you can outsource from the beginning of starting your business, as well as write or video the process used so you are ready to train them quickly when they come on board.

It is understandable to want to save money on tasks that you can easily do yourself, like administrative tasks. You may also be afraid to spend money hiring someone for the tasks that you aren't great at, because the business isn't making enough money yet. Let's, however, take a closer look at your options. Are you spending hours on your business doing these $10 tasks when you can bill more than that per hour for your services (i.e., $199 and above per hour)? If so, you are limiting the success of your business and for every hour that you spend on those $10 tasks, you are actually *losing* money.

The important concept to understand is that these $10 tasks don't only cost you $10. Instead, the "real" cost of these tasks is equal to Your Yield Per Hour minus the Cost of Task. Therefore, if you can make $250 per hour and a particular task can be outsourced for $10 per hour, the *opportunity cost* (revenue "lost") of doing this task yourself is $240.

If you are excited about outsourcing these $10 tasks, but don't know where to find someone to do this, one great resource is a site called Upwork. I have had great experiences hiring freelancers to help me create custom .pdf files and do data entry for less than $10 per hour. Another popular site to find freelancers is Fiverr.

CASE STUDIES

Here are two real-life examples of outsourcing tasks.

Customer Intake Form Completed in Less Than One Business Day

I had agonized and tried for weeks to create a customized customer intake form in Microsoft Word that would allow users to fill-out basic profile information and email the information back to me. When certain customers who didn't have a scanner tried to fill out the form directly in Word, the formatting made it difficult to read. After several clients didn't complete and send the forms ahead of their initial meeting, I decided to hire someone to create an editable form in Adobe Acrobat. Based on recommendations from colleagues, I used a freelancer site called Upwork. I created a profile, posted a job description of the project, and had candidates applying within minutes of the job posting. Next, I interviewed and selected a freelancer – all within 2 hours of posting the job. On a Friday night, I sent my freelancer the information needed to create and fix my file. By Monday morning, I received a completed project with an intake form that enabled clients to enter information directly into an editable .pdf and click a button to save, print, and email directly back to me!

Virtual Assistant And Personal Assistant Free Up Your Time

Productivity Coach Marcey Rader, employs a full-time virtual technical assistant in the Philippines. One of her favorite things to do in the morning is to look at the app badge on her phone with the number of tasks her assistant completed (working in a different time zone) while she was asleep!

Rader encourages her clients to do quick videos and record the steps for blog posting, administrative tasks, or anything else that can be documented and put them into an electronic manual so any assistant can quickly jump on board and complete the work to specifications, without wasting time re-training.

If you aren't ready to hire a virtual assistant, consider hiring a personal assistant to help you with tasks around the house, like laundry, cleaning, errand-running, and cooking, to free up more time for your business. Rader recommends Care.com to find exactly what you need. Think outside the typical box of a housecleaning service. Her personal assistant preps her meals, does laundry, sews, and cleans different parts of her house each week.

The Bottom Line

By recognizing that you can't afford to do certain tasks because your yield per hour is significantly greater than the cost to hire someone else, you can become more confident in knowing when to *outsource* the tasks that you don't like and in some cases, shouldn't be doing anyway. Instead of viewing something as a $10 task, look at it from the opportunity cost of your potential income minus the cost of the $10 task. If you are not ready to outsource tasks in your business, you can also start by hiring someone to help you with personal tasks around the house to free up time so you can spend on business. Get started today in researching how to off-load these tasks so you can focus on what you're good at and what can generate more income!

Complete the following template to calculate your yield per hour to know when you can afford to hire help.

Template: Know When to Hire Help

Action Steps

1. Take an inventory of all the tasks that you do for your business.
2. Next, write down (or research) how much would it cost you to outsource that task.

What are the activities in your business?	How much would it cost for have someone else do this activity?
1.	$
2.	$
3.	$
4.	$
5.	$

3. Now, determine your yield per hour, which is how much income you need to produce for each hour you work. This is determined by answering (and calculating) the following:

   A. **What is your target annual income? $__________**

   B. **How many weeks per year do you want to work? ________ weeks**

   C. **How many hours per week do you want to work? ________ hours**

   D. **Your Yield per Hour is (A ÷ (B × C)) = $ _________**

4. Finally, compare the cost of an activity to your yield per hour. If the cost is less than your yield per hour, stop doing it or hire someone else to do it for you!

   If Yield Per Hour > Cost of Task… Stop doing it or Outsource

   If Yield Per Hour < Cost of Task….Do it yourself

   **Calculating your yield per hour formula made available from Team Nimbus of North Carolina, LLC.*

Part III

Protect With A Strong Roof

"At the end of the day, the goals are simple: safety and security."

—Jodi Rell

Chapter 16

Protect Your Family and Business

This chapter is not to be used as your source of legal advice. It is meant to share areas for consideration to protect your family and business, and avoid putting your personal assets at risk.

Have you registered your business as a limited liability company (LLC)? If it's not an LLC, is it an S-Corp, or C-Corp? If your business is not registered as one of these options, you are putting your personal assets and family at risk. Many people make the mistake of thinking that their business isn't big enough yet or has little risk of being sued, especially if they are in direct sales or are being hired as an independent consultant. Whether a person sues you or not, is not always your fault or the result of your behavior. Then there are those who just don't want to pay the fees associated with registering and maintaining an LLC or corporation. It is a big mistake, however, to avoid creating a legal entity that could protect your personal assets and shift liability to your business. After all, it is the business engaging in the activity, so why would you not want the business to shoulder the risk? A lawsuit does not mean that the business did anything wrong. It simply means someone has chosen to sue the business or you. Insurance policies such as liability, disability, and life insurance should also be considered to protect your finances. Take the necessary steps now to protect your income and your business so that one lawsuit, injury, or unexpected death does not put you out of business and have you wondering where you will get the money to pay your next bills.

	*Tip: Did you know that a single member LLC is treated like a sole proprietor in the eyes of the IRS? While for tax purposes they are treated the same, a sole proprietorship is not a legal entity.*

Tip: Whether a person sues you or not, is not always your fault or the result of your behavior. Whether the other person will win the suit or not will depend on what he or she can prove in court.

If someone decides to sue you, your personal assets (including home, car, and personal bank accounts) are at risk if you are a sole proprietor. If there is not enough money in the business to pay the settlement, then your personal assets are taken to pay the remaining balance.

Insurance Policies

In addition to the legal entity, you need to consider insurance policies. Check with an insurance agent on recommended insurance policies including general liability insurance and professional liability insurance, also known as errors & omissions (E&O). Seek help from a financial advisor to identify the amount of disability insurance needed in the event that you are disabled and can't perform the duties necessary to continue working. Some financial advisors can also assist you in obtaining disability insurance to ensure you protect the income required to support yourself and the family.

Last, but not least, you may want to consider applying for a life insurance policy to ensure the business can continue in the event that you (the owner), partner, or key employee dies. *A business can quickly deteriorate if an owner, partner, or key employee passes away.* Getting a life insurance policy can provide the surviving business partners enough capital and time to look for a replacement or buy out the heirs of the deceased. A financial advisor or insurance agent can help you run scenarios to determine how much life insurance and what type – term or permanent life insurance – that you should obtain. Financial advisors are extremely knowledgeable as to which companies will provide the best policies and rates given your particular situation and health history. If you leave your corporate job to work on your business full-time, your personal group life insurance will go away when you leave, so investigate getting coverage prior to making any major changes.

Direct Sales Representatives and Independent Consultants

While you may believe that you don't have any legal risks of being sued because products are shipped directly to the customer, why take that chance? I have consulted both a CPA and business lawyer to see if there are any exceptions for those in direct sales, and they found none. In fact, the CPA pointed out that one client in direct sales set up her business as an LLC, especially because she will enter other people's home to showcase the products. If something happens during one of these hostess parties, she doesn't want the exposure to a potential lawsuit.

It is critical to plan for the one percent chance that something goes wrong and not place your personal assets in jeopardy. Take the time to set-up your business correctly from the beginning and avoid any regrets later.

Commonly asked questions if you are thinking, there may be exceptions to needing an LLC.

1. **What if I'm in direct sales and there really isn't any personal liability? I have products that get shipped directly to the customer and there is very little risk.**

   Every business attorney and CPA that I have consulted said that they can think of many reasons why you should still set up an LLC. What if the product you sell is ingested and harms a child or pet? What if the customer has an allergic reaction? Sure, the customer is more likely to sue the big company, but why not take the simple steps to add a layer of protection in case they adopt a "sue everyone" model? It is safer to set-up an LLC to protect your personal assets, including home, car, and personal bank accounts.

   Please consult a lawyer and CPA to get specific advice for your business and personal situation.

2. **What if I think this will complicate things? I don't want to add unnecessary work and increase my tax fees by setting up an LLC.**

   Yes, there are steps that you have to take in order to form an LLC, but the steps aren't complicated once you know what you have to do and when you have to do them. You do have to open separate bank accounts as discussed in Chapter 1: Separate Personal and Business Expenses in order to separate the personal and business expenses. You will also have to file an annual report and pay the renewal fee.

3. **What if I don't know how to create an annual report? I'm not good with numbers.**

   Don't worry, the annual report for an LLC isn't the same type of annual report you're probably thinking of that includes a company's balance sheet, income statement, and other financial data that businesses usually have to produce for shareholders. The state government is typically wanting to verify that your LLC is still operating, the current business address, registration information, and names of people in the company.

4. **What if I don't know if I can afford all the fees associated with having an LLC?**

   There is a one-time formation fee to form a corporation or LLC, which shouldn't have a significant impact over the lifetime of your business. The annual filing fees vary by state. If you mark your calendar for when your annual filings are due and pay on time, you can avoid any late filing fees or reinstatement fees if your LLC is put on administrative hold for late payment.

   Tax preparation for a sole proprietor and an LLC is the same; both are documented on the Schedule C (Form 1040), so there are no extra tax preparation fees. Check with your CPA to understand tax implications if you incorporate in one state, but have clients in other states.

Tip: While it is called an LLC annual report, in some states, it actually isn't due every year. At the time of this writing, some states, such as Iowa and Indiana only require that LLCs file every other year. Pennsylvania only requires every 10 years. Then some states like North Carolina, Florida, and Delaware mandate it to be filed every year.

5. **What if I already have an $1 Million umbrella policy on top of my personal home insurance policy that should cover any issues?**

   It comes down to what your risk tolerance is and what the potential is that someone could sue you for more than your coverage. Also, you should confirm if a personal policy will cover a business liability issue. Remember, a sole proprietorship is not a legal entity. Your personal assets including home, car, and bank accounts could be liable in the event you are ever sued. You have to ask yourself, "Could I afford it if someone were to ever sue me for over one million dollars?"

6. **What if I decide that I'm going to leave my business as a sole proprietorship. What else should I be aware of?**

   Eric G., a CPA, said that he advises those clients who decide that they still want to do a sole proprietorship to apply for a separate tax identification number. This way, they decrease the risks of identity theft by having an employer identification number (EIN) and are not giving out their social security number whenever they submit W-9 forms.

Tip: If anyone pays you over $600 for services, they will request that you complete a W-9 form in order to submit a Form 1099-MISC. Similarly, if you pay someone over $600 for services, you should request a completed W-9 form.

7. **What if getting a separate tax identification number complicates my taxes? I don't want to have to pay the CPA more money.**

   Having a separate tax identification number for your business will not complicate your taxes or cost more money. On the Schedule C (Form 1040) and Form W-9, there are places to provide both your social security number and employer identification number.

8. **What if I decide to get an employer identification number (EIN) but I've already started my business under my social security number (SSN)? Doesn't that complicate my taxes and increase my tax fees?**

   Eric G., a CPA I consulted, said there shouldn't be any additional fees as your CPA will just enter both your social security number and employer identification number on the Schedule C (Form 1040) and Form W-9. Then, he or she will add up the total numbers from the 1099s under your SSN and EIN. (*Note – If you decide to do your taxes, it is the same process but I highly recommend small business owners to work with a CPA to do their small business taxes.)

   A limited liability company (LLC) is one of the easier entities to form that keeps the business separate from the personal. If anything were to happen with the business and there were not enough assets in the business to pay off debts or pay a lawsuit, then the person suing could only get as much as what the business owns.

If you haven't set-up your legal entity and you are now convinced that you need one, then:

1. Decide on and register the business name.
2. Form your legal entity with Secretary of State.
3. Apply for a tax identification number for the business, also called EIN.
4. Open business bank accounts and credit card.

For those who haven't started or registered their business.

When choosing a business name, be sure to do an online search to understand if there are any similar businesses operating under that name. First step is to do a quick online search. Second step is to go to your Secretary of State site and do a search. If you really want to be careful and be 100% certain, you can pay a business lawyer or trademark lawyer to do a more extensive search for you.

CASE STUDIES

Selecting Your Business Name Is Important

Cease and Desist

One of my business mentors shared a story that happened to one of his small business clients that shows the importance of selecting your business name and the pitfalls if a bigger, global company believes that your company name is too similar to theirs.

Chris T., the small business owner, received a letter from a Fortune 500 company saying that the name of his company was too similar to theirs and they gave him a cease and desist order of using his business name. In return, they would not sue him and gave him $400 for the "trouble." As a small business owner, Chris didn't have the resources to fight the case or even re-brand the business with marketing efforts of a new website, logo, business cards, etc. He took the $400 and shut down his business. Chris later created a completely new company with a different name.

Upsetting the Competition

Early in her business, Helen Moses, owner of Command Communication, PLLC got an email from another business owner who was upset that Helen created a website domain name that was too similar to hers. The only thing different was one letter in the website URL and the other owner was afraid that it would cause confusion for customers. Helen was only checking for business names with the word "communication" in the singular form and since her original choice was taken, she bought the domain with a hyphen and owns www.command-communication.com. However, this other business owned www.command-communications.com in the plural form. Do you see the potential confusion? After looking through the other owner's site, it was obvious that the two businesses were not direct competitors. The owners came to an agreement and understanding that worked for them. At the time of this writing, the other website is no longer active.

Here is example of when a business owner didn't set up a separate entity to provide the added layer of protection and exposed herself to personal liability.

Sole Proprietor

Calley Gerber, an animal lawyer in Raleigh, NC, shared some scenarios with me based upon her experience. She provided the following hypothetical situation to illustrate the point:

Example: Susie Smith is a professional dog walker. One day while walking a client's dog, the dog attacks a cat hiding under a bush. After thousands in veterinary bills, the owner of the cat files a lawsuit against the owner of the dog as well as Susie, who was exercising control over the dog at the time of the attack. In addition, the owner of the dog may try to assert a claim against Susie for not using reasonable care and due diligence to notice the cat and prevent the attack. If Susie had registered her business as an LLC, her personal assets would be protected. However, by operating as a sole proprietor, Susie left her personal assets, including home and car, vulnerable in a lawsuit.

Tip: Did you know that if you register your business as an LLC, you may not have a full year before you owe annual filing fees? Be sure to check the due dates of annual reports in the state that you registered your business, as that may affect when you want to register.

Be sure to mark your calendar for the due dates of annual report filing. You may not always have a full year before you have to file. For example, annual reports are due by April 15th in North Carolina. If you registered your business in North Carolina and paid the $125 initial filing fee on December 15th, you will have to file the first annual report and pay the $200 annual report fee plus $2 electronic filing fee by April 15th of the following year. It doesn't matter that you were only open for business for two weeks.

If you are not sure of the steps to form a legal entity, there are business lawyers who can properly form one with the correct documentation, including articles of organization, operating agreement, and partnership agreement. If you want to create an LLC, some lawyers will help you confirm the availability of your desired business name, submit the proper documentation to form the LLC with the Secretary of State, write the articles of organization, and provide your EIN for a flat fee.

Your business must have its own tax identification number. The tax identification number should *not* be your social security number. Having a separate tax identification number for the business, also called a federal employer identification number (EIN), will allow you to keep your social security number private and secure. Whenever you pay any contractors more than $600 for work, you will need to send them a 1099 form with your tax identification number. Protect your personal life by keeping it separate from the business and apply for the EIN that is only associated with the business.

Tip: Did you know if that if you are late paying the annual fee for your LLC, that your business may be put on administrative hold by your state, and you may lose all legal protection until the business is re-instated? If anyone sues your business during that holding period, you could be personally liable!

The Bottom Line

This book is not meant to be used as your source of legal advice. It is meant to make you aware as to the inherent danger of allowing your personal assets, such as your home, car, and personal bank accounts, to be at risk in the event of a lawsuit, when there are options to create a business entity. With an LLC, as example, the risk is limited to only the business assets. Also, check out liability and disability insurance policies because a business structure alone is not enough protection.

The fees for initial filing and annual reports for an LLC vary by state. If your business can not afford to pay the annual fee for the basic legal protection, then look into decreasing expenses or increasing income. Protect your family and business so you can sleep better at night, because as Benjamin Franklin once said, "If you fail to plan, you are planning to fail!"

Refer to the template following this chapter to research all the applicable fees in starting and maintaining your business.

Tip: Did you know that in the state of Florida, if you are late paying your annual report filing fee, the late fee is $400?!? Mark your calendar to pay your annual fees on time.

Template: Research Fees In Starting and Maintaining Business

Legal Entity			
Fees			
Formation Fees *(one-time)*			
Annual Fee			
Annual Filing Date			
Franchise tax *(some states impose this in place of, or on top of, the annual report filing fee and state income tax)*			
State Corporate Income Tax			
Late Fee *(if annual filing is late)*			
Reinstatement Fee *(if put on administrative hold due to late filing)*			
Dissolution fee *(if and when dissolve business)*			

Chapter 17

Build a Cash Cushion for Greater Flexibility

While many large corporations borrow money, don't automatically assume that as a small business owner that you have to borrow or use a credit card to run your business. Yes, sometimes it takes money to make money. However, it is much better to have cash than to go into debt and not be able to pay your bills. Lack of cash is one of the top reasons that many small businesses fail. Consider building up a sizeable cash cushion prior to starting your business if you are still in the planning phases.

Let's take a look at two examples of small business owners and how outstanding *invoices* affect their cash flow differently:

Late Larry is constantly behind on paying his bills and is frustrated. He has several reliable customers who pay him on time, but others who he has to chase down so he is often paid two weeks to a month behind. This causes a lot of stress for him as he relies on customers to pay invoices on time in order to have enough cash to pay his own bills. Unfortunately, he has now been late paying his business credit card three times this year. In addition to the late fees, he also incurred interest.

Cash Carrie has three months of cash reserve in her business savings account. She only purchases inventory and hires services when she already has the cash in her account. While she does invoice her own customers and gives them 30 days to pay, she is not relying on them to pay those bills in order to make her own current bills. Essentially, she runs a cash-based business since she pays a bill directly from her business checking account.

	Late Larry	Cash Carrie
Accounts Receivable (aka outstanding client invoices to be paid)	$500	$500
Accounts Payable (aka outstanding bills owed)	$500	N/A – paid on-time
Late Fees ($25 each)	$25 x 3 = $75	N/A
Interest	$575 x 25.3% (compounded daily)	N/A

Steps to Creating Enough Cash

1. If you are just starting your business, be sure to research and calculate the start-up expenses. Make sure you have enough cash to pay for these start-up expenses. (*Note – Start-up expenses should be part of the financial plan created. Refer to Chapter 2: Predict Your Financial Success if you did not create one.)
2. Next, list all the monthly and yearly expenses. (*Note – If you don't know how to create a budget, this will be discussed in more detail in Chapter 18: Plan for Every Dollar Earned.)
3. Calculate the average monthly costs.
4. Make sure you have at least one month of cash reserves to pay for the average monthly costs. If you don't, make a plan to start saving and putting this cash reserve in your business savings account.
5. Next, work to create a 3 – 6 months' cash reserve depending on your business model to minimize business failure due to unforeseen circumstances or slower sales months.
6. If there are issues with clients paying invoices on-time, consider switching to a business model where they have to pay upfront before you provide services or ship products. Refer to Chapter 13: Collect on Outstanding Invoices if you are having issues with collecting payments from customers.
7. If you are already in debt, create a plan to pay off the debt as quickly as possible. This may mean cutting back on expenses to free up cash.

CASE STUDY

Here is a real-life client story where lack of cash meant turning down work

Chelsea S. was a preferred vendor for a company conducting training events and was required to travel to different office locations to train the company's staff. There were several times when she was asked to travel out of state, which required a flight. While she really wanted to accept the job and needed the money, Chelsea had to turn it down because she didn't have the cash to pre-pay for her travel expenses. It was an unfortunate cycle because she really needed the work and money. She commanded between $1,000 - $1,500 per workshop, and because she couldn't afford to book a $300 flight and $200 hotel and wait for two to three weeks to be reimbursed for travel expenses, she had to turn down work.

If Chelsea had enough of a cash cushion, she would be able to confidently accept the job offers and make the money she needed to sustain and grow her business.

Often, business owners make the mistake of quitting their day job too early to spend more time on their business. That can be a risky choice when the business has not proven itself yet. If you have the luxury of time on your side to plan in advance before starting your business (meaning you didn't get laid off), it is recommended you not quit your day job until your business has shown consistent profit margins that allows it to pay the required *income* you need to support your lifestyle. If you need more cash to start your business, one option is to stop contributing to your company 401k and put any extra money into the business savings.

CASE STUDIES

Reduced Hours At Corporate Job

During one of my presentations to a group of aspiring business owners, Tiffany A. shared with the group that she almost made the mistake of quitting her corporate job because she was sleep-deprived from spending late nights working on her new business after she got home from work. She didn't, however, have a cash cushion to support herself for the undetermined time it would take her to finish planning her business and start making money.

Instead, she approached the company to see if she could decrease her number of hours, and was able to reduce her hours by 10 hours per week and still maintain her full-time status to receive benefits. It was a win-win for her, her future business, and her company.

Ditched brick and mortar business to save almost $50,000 in first year

One aspiring entrepreneur shared with me that after listening to my advice to have a cash cushion at a small business presentation, she re-evaluated her current business plan and start-up expenses. Vivian had planned to apply for a $25,000 bank loan to pay for start-up costs and to sign a lease in downtown for $2,000 per month for a brick and mortar space to open her beauty salon.

Now, she is modifying her business plan to start off as a mobile business and to go to the customer's location (e.g., retirement communities and hospitals), to build a cash cushion prior to committing to a lease in the city. In addition to the $25,000 bank loan and interest fees, she is saving $24,000 each year by not committing to a fixed cost of rent.

The Bottom Line

If you start using a credit card to pay for start-up expenses before your first paying client, it can create a dangerous cycle of incurring late fees and paying interest because you can't guarantee when you will secure your first paying client or when your clients will pay. Similarly, if you try to expand your business too quickly and take on debt to do so, this can also start a debt cycle that can be hard to break.

To avoid paying interest or late fees, creating enough cash cushion (recommended at least three months of expenses) can help during those slow months or with unexpected emergencies and trailing accounts receivables.

If the numbers and calculations seem too complex and you are not sure how you can create a cash cushion with your current business debt, contact a financial coach to help create a debt elimination plan with you.

Chapter 18

Plan for Every Dollar Earned

Many of us cringe when we hear the word *budget*. For some it's restrictive, like a diet, and in many cases people avoid doing one at all. You've likely looked at your bank account balance at the end of the month and at least once wondered, "Where did all the money go?!?" It is easy to see money coming in from all the sales each month, yet then we get the surprise that there is not much leftover after paying all the bills. If you do not have a good handle on where your money is going, then it is time to start tracking it. Once you know where the money goes, you can start a plan for where you want it to *start* going — otherwise known as a budget. We can decide to re-program our mind to view the word "budget" as a future plan for every dollar that we earn. If we view a budget as a tool that enables us to plan ahead and designate how we want the money in our business to be spent, then we realize that a budget actually gives us more control and freedom to buy what we need and want.

For Start-up Expenses

If you haven't started your business yet, consider the one-time fees to set-up your business, including security deposits, insurance, legal professional fees, licenses, registration costs, expenses incurred prior to launch of your business, and capital expenditures. All of these expenses should be in your business and financial plan. NOTE: Refer to Chapter 2: Predict Your Financial Success if you don't have a financial plan.

For Operating Expenses

You want to forecast how much you will spend each month for the entire year. This should include recurring, one-time, and annual expenses. The level of detail that you track will depend on your business needs and the IRS Schedule C (Form 1040) Profit or Loss From Business is a great place to start as a reference for expenses that you may be able deduct.

Here are categories to get you started. Refer to Schedule C (Form 1040) for the complete list of business deductions.

- Advertising
- Bank Charges
- Dues & Subscriptions
- Insurance
- Licenses and Fees
- Marketing and Promotion
- Meals & Entertainment
- Office Expenses
- Office Supplies
- Payroll Expenses
- Professional Fees
- Property Taxes
- Rent
- Repairs and Maintenance
- Shipping & Delivery
- Telephone
- Training & Development
- Travel
- Utilities
- Vehicle (*only if company owns the vehicle)
- Other

Some items like dues and subscriptions may only be billed once a year. There you will note variance in the total operating expenses per month. As discussed in Chapter 9: Don't Go Broke Over Monthly and Yearly Obligations, make sure you have a list of due dates for these annual dues and subscriptions so you are setting aside that money and there are no surprises later.

Creating a budget can be as simple as entering the list of expenses in a spreadsheet with the total that you predict you will spend each month in each category. If this is your first time creating a budget, it may take a couple of hours to gather the information to make an educated guess on how much you plan to spend. You can reference data from prior months to get a starting point on a realistic number, and adjust as needed.

The Bottom Line

Creating and managing a budget is necessary to understand how to forecast income and expenses for your business and determine if you need to make changes due to previous month's or year's performance. If you don't create a budget or have one that isn't really accurate, you may find yourself quickly spending more money than is coming in and accruing debt at the same time. Eventually, this debt will lead to business failure since you can't operate a business if you can't pay your bills.

Remember to consider fixed, variable, and annual expenses when creating a budget. You can avoid a common mistake by setting aside the time to review your budget prior to each month and fiscal year.

Chapter 19

Use the Past to Understand What to Change

To maximize your business success, make changes, and to continue to grow, you need insight into your past business financials to see if there are any patterns that are not working and decide what to do next. Examples may be cutting costs, raising prices, creating promotions, or eliminating a product offering. To do this, you must put together your Profit and Loss Statement.

The Profit and Loss Statement, commonly referred to as P&L, is one of the most important financial statements to help you understand if changes need to be made in your business. It reflects whether you are making more money than you are spending and gives you an overview of your total revenues, cost of sales, total expenses, and *net profit(s)* [or loss(s)] are. If you have been incurring high cost of sales and net loss for several months in a row, having this financial information helps you make informed decisions. The P&L also provides the data needed for CPAs to prepare your taxes.

For those of you who are not accounting majors and dislike numbers, here is an overview of the terminology for what you input into the P&L:

Revenue. This is the income that a business receives from the sale of goods and services. It is also referred to as ***Sales*** or ***Income***.

Cost of Sales. This is the cost to create a product or service that has been sold. This can also be known as ***Cost of Goods Sold or COGS***. NOTE: Service providers tend to use the term cost of sales and manufacturers and retailers tend to use the term cost of goods sold.

Gross Profit. This is calculated as Total Revenue minus Total Cost of Sales.

Expenses. These are ***costs*** incurred to operate the business and provide products and services. They include fixed (i.e., overhead expenses) and variable costs.

Net Profit. This is calculated as Gross Profits minus Total Expenses. If this number is positive, there is net income. If negative, there is a loss.

Profit & Loss Statement (P&L). This shows the net income or loss the business has incurred over a period of time. Also referred as ***Income Statement***.

Tracking Expenses

To calculate expenses, decide how you want to track them. Do you like spreadsheets? Or do you prefer an automated tool or phone app? When you are just starting out, spreadsheets is all you need. If soon you have hundreds of transactions per month or if you're not a fan of spreadsheets, a paid subscription for an automated tool can be worthwhile if it can keep you on track and captures accurate information that can be provided to your CPA.

Option 1: Spreadsheet. This is one of the least expensive options, since most of us already have a spreadsheet tool like Excel or access to Google sheets. It is however more manual and time-consuming.

Example: You can download all the debit and credit card transactions for a specific period (i.e., June 1st – June 30th), then go through them and enter or update any default categories that the bank or credit card associated with the expenses.

Option 2: Tools. There are many accounting tools available, such as QuickBooks and FreshBooks, that can import data and attempt to automatically assign categories to your expenses. (These two tools also have invoicing and payment features, which we learned in Chapter 8: Collect Money to Stay in Business is important.) The tools can automatically organize your expenses online if you grant computer access to your bank and credit card accounts.

When evaluating tools, decide if you need a single-entry system or double-entry system to track income and expenses. Single-entry systems are easy. You simply enter each transaction once, designating it as income or expense. If, however, you have to track inventory, loans, assets, and liabilities, go with a double-entry system. Double-entry systems will require each transaction to be first entered as a debit and a second time as an equal credit, which creates a balance.

Tip: FreshBooks is a single-entry system and is good if you don't have a lot of transactions. QuickBooks is better for businesses that track inventory, loans, assets, and liabilities because it is a double-entry system.

CASE STUDY

My Personal Real-Life Example:

I am currently using Freshbooks to automatically import my bank transactions. One of my charges at the post office was automatically categorized as "Office Expenses & Postage" with the date of the transaction and amount. There was no additional work necessary on my part.

On the other hand, my monthly email marketing subscription to MailChimp was uncategorized. The system marked it as "Uncategorized," so I went in to edit the details by:

1. Entering Vendor = MailChimp
2. Category = Marketing

There is a feature that allows you to check if this expense is recurring, and if so, the frequency. Then you can select to "Remember this category for similar expenses." By checking this box, the system should start to recognize this type of expense from this vendor going forward, and will categorize it correctly, so you don't have to manually go in and edit the details every time.

Within Freshbooks, you can override and correct or add additional information to each expense such as:

- Vendor
- Category
- Notes

Example: For coffee purchased at Caribou Coffee during a consultation meeting with Joe Smith, I added the following details:

- Vendor = *Caribou Coffee*
- *Category = (no action necessary as it was correctly flagged as "Dining and Meals")*
- *Notes* = Consultation Session with Joe Smith

Downside — Too Many Expenses

Even if your business makes a lot of money in sales, the important thing to any creditor is the bottom line — your net profits. If your expenses are too high and your business shows little to no profit and you take little to no owner's draw, that can affect your ability to obtain credit or get approved for a personal mortgage.

One personal banker shared with me that small business owners often are surprised that they are declined for a mortgage because their debt-to-income ratio is too high. The small business owners will try to point out that business is extremely successful and will show the sales figures, and then realize the important number is the net profit.

If your Profit & Loss Statement shows only a $1,000 in net profit each month, then the bank is likely to not approve you for a $300,000 mortgage, because at most you are only able to take out $12,000 in owner's draw.

The Bottom Line

Once you have set-up a good tracking system for your expenses, it will be easier to create a monthly, quarterly, and yearly P&L Statement to spot trends and see how much you are spending in each category. You might well be surprised to learn how much you are spending in certain categories, especially Meals & Entertainment or Dues and Subscriptions. By using the Profit and Loss Statement to understand your financial history, you can understand what to change when creating a future budget.

Refer to the template provided at the end of the chapter to get started on creating a P&L.

For links to resources and ready-to-use templates referenced in this chapter, visit www.smallbusinessfinancebook.com/kit and enter your email address to gain instant access.

Template: Create Profit & Loss Statement

	Jan	Feb	Mar	Total
Revenue (Sales)				
<Product 1>				
<Product 2>				
Total Revenue (Sales)				
Cost of Sales				
<Product 1>				
<Product 2>				
Total Cost of Sales				
Gross Profit				
Expenses				
Advertising				
Commissions & Fees				
Contract Labor				
Depreciation				
Insurance				
Legal & Professional Services				
Office Expense				
Rent or lease				
Repairs and maintenance				
Supplies				
Taxes & Licenses				
Travel				
Meals & Entertainment				
Utilities				
Wages				
Other Expenses				
Total Expenses				
Net Profit	0	0	0	0

Chapter 20

Become More Confident in Business Decisions

For those of you who aren't accounting majors, you may not fully understand the effects that your sales prices, costs, and the number of hours worked have on your ability to stay in business. This is where many small business owners make a major mistake. You have to know what the break-even point is to understand how many products you need to sell to break-even on costs. Otherwise, you may not realize that you are actually losing money for every product sold because you didn't make this calculation.

The formula to calculate the break-even point per month:

Break-Even point = Overhead Expenses ÷ (Sales price per unit – Direct Costs per unit)

	*Tip: Adjust the sales price or the fixed costs if the break-even point is not realistic.*

Let's look at two different business owners and determine how many clients or products they need to sell each month to break-even on their costs.

Coach Chad has a coaching business and charges $200 per coaching session. He has overhead costs of $500 per month for rent, telephone, and dues and subscriptions, and wants to pay himself $80 for each session.

Production Paul has a production plant and sells pens. He has an overhead cost of $2,000 per month for rent, telephone, salary, and insurance. He sells his pens at $1 per unit and it costs him $0.30 to make each pen.

Coach Chad

Overhead Costs = $500

Sales price per coaching session = $200

Direct Cost = $80

Break-Even: $500 / ($200 - $80) = 4.16

Conclusion: **Coach Chad** needs to have 5 coaching sessions (since he can't do 0.16 of a session) in order to break even each month.

Production Paul

Overhead Costs = $2,000

Sales price per pen = $1.00

Direct Cost = $0.30

Break Even = $2,000 / ($1.00 - $0.30) = 2,857.1

Conclusion: **Production Paul** would have to sell 2,858 pens (since he can't sell 0.1 of a pen) in order to break-even each month.

Now, let's see what happens in the following two scenarios if Production Paul wants to know what would happen if he could cut his direct costs by 50% versus raise his price by 50%. Which is the better business decision?

Scenario 1

Production Paul looks to cut costs by 50% and finds that he can get it down to $0.15 per pen. His new break-even point is:

$2,000 / ($1.00 - $.15) = 2,353 pens

Scenario 2

If **Production Paul** decides to raise the price of his pen to $1.50, he would need to sell the following number of pens to break-even:

$2,000 / ($1.50 - $0.30) = 1,667 pens

What do you think Production Paul should do – cut his costs or raise his prices?

The Bottom Line

It is important to understand exactly how many products you need to sell or clients that you need to see in order to break-even each month based on your pricing and costs. Once you calculate the break-even point, you may realize that you need to change your prices or decrease costs. In order to become or stay profitable, you need to understand these numbers to make informed business decisions. Without these numbers, you may find yourself trying to meet unrealistic goals and going into debt when you can't meet the required sales to just break even.

Activity: Determine How Many Products You Need to Sell or Clients You Need

Deliverable: Break-even Point Analysis

Time Required: 30 minutes – 1 hour

Steps:

1. Calculate overhead costs per month: ____________________
2. Enter sales price per unit: ____________________________
3. Enter direct costs per unit: ___________________________
4. Calculate break-even point:

   Overhead costs / (Sales Price – Direct Costs)

   ________ / (__________ - ________) = __________________
5. Does your break-even point surprise you? Write down any thoughts and business decisions you want to make:

   ____

   ____
6. If you aren't happy with the number you calculated in Step 4, go on to analyze two other scenarios by adjusting price and/or costs:

   Scenario 1:

   Overhead costs / (Sales Price – Direct Costs)
   ________ / (__________ - ________) = __________________

   Scenario 2:

   Overhead costs / (Sales Price – Direct Costs)

   ________ / (__________ - ________) = __________________
7. Write down any thoughts or business decisions based on the scenarios you just created.

   ____

   ____

Part IV
Make Improvements

"Continuous improvement is better than delayed perfection."

—Mark Twain

Chapter 21

Accelerate Success by Leveraging Others' Expertise

Have you thought to yourself, "I don't know, what I don't know?" Every successful business owner will likely tell you that they could not have done it alone. I completely agree. We all have our strengths and core competencies and are all starting at different points on the entrepreneurship learning curve. When you know that you do not and cannot know everything there is to know about running a profitable business, then you are more likely to succeed by reaching out for help.

Many of you will initially seek to learn from the traditional methods like paying for a business planning course, reading a book, or doing online searches. Other times, you will seek out professionals like CPAs and business lawyers. Sometimes you are fortunate enough to find mentors, colleagues, and accountability partners who motivate you and share their expertise and experience. I did all of these same things similar to you, however, the group that I really did not have a good handle on when I entered the small business world is coaches.

Do you know how a coach can help you with your business? The word "coach" can be a very broad term, yet essentially it is a person who motivates and trains someone to accomplish a goal or task. Most successful athletes understand the importance and power of coaching. Many companies also invest in coaching for their executives and high performers. As a small business owner, hiring a coach can help you achieve the results that you want and need in your business, especially if you need to get clear about your goals, identify your weak spots, be accountable, have a sounding board, and gain a competitive advantage. How much is achieving success worth to you? Or better yet, what will happen to your business if you don't achieve your goals?

Hiring a coach should be viewed as an investment, rather than an expense. During my first year of business, I met different types of coaches and had no idea that these kind of specialized expertise existed. I have hired several of these coaches and have told them that I wish that I knew that they existed ... six months prior! Had I known then what I know now, I could have hired them sooner and saved myself a lot of late nights at the computer trying to figure out how to do it on my own. In particular, a good business or financial coach can help make sure you aren't wasting your time, have a viable service and product, and are on the right path. Finding and budgeting for the right resources to help you with your business is critical to your chances of success.

There are a wide variety of coaches providing services and education in their areas of expertise. Did you know that there are coaches and consultants who can teach you how to:

- Be more intentional at networking so you can gain more clients.
- Master the client acquisition process so customers are moving themselves through the buying process, as opposed to you selling to them like a salesman.
- Be more productive while traveling for business.
- Work effectively with virtual assistants across the globe.
- Learn how to get your inbox down to zero emails at the end of each day.
- Be a better presenter and keep the audience engaged with your voice.
- Create effective marketing campaigns to help you launch your first book to Amazon best seller status.
- Understand the numbers in order to become more confident and profitable in running your business.

Now that you know that these coaches and services exist, identify any gaps in your current business skills and knowledge, then budget to hire a coach to help you move your business where you want it to be. If you don't know providers of these services, reach out to your business network or check out professional networking groups.

There are also mastermind groups. I first heard this term at one of my financial conferences at the beginning stages of my business and I had no idea how to find or join mastermind group. I felt completely left out and not in the know. Essentially a mastermind is a group of like-minded people who offer brainstorming, education, peer accountability, and support in a group setting to help each member achieve success. There is an expected commitment and participation required. Almost every successful business owner that I've met is a member of a mastermind group. Some of these groups will charge a few hundred dollars a month, some will charge up to a few thousand dollars a month, and some are free. If you are lucky to be invited to a mastermind group or find a good one, consider budgeting to join and participate to grow yourself and your business.

Next Success Steps

If you come from the corporate world, you've likely figured out that being a small business owner is an entirely different ball game. Things you learned in college and the corporate world do not equip you with what you need to know to run your business effectively from a financial perspective. Colleges tend to teach you how to be a good employee for a company. They don't teach you the skills to be the employer and how to grow and run an entire business from the ground up. As someone who graduated with a business major and worked for a global IT consulting firm, primarily focused on the financial service industry, I know this from personal experience. In fact, over 90% of what you have discovered in this book is information I acquired over time and after many hours searching through the Internet, reading start-up business books, paying for small business courses, asking mentors and colleagues, paying for certified professionals at over $200 per hour ... and by learning on the job, running my own service-based business. There are several things that I learned the hard way or wished that I had known sooner. It would have been great to have all this information in the first year of my business to all be housed in one place.

The great news is that if this seems overwhelming and stressful, help is only a click away! The fastest way to get started on the path of understanding how to ensure your company is safe and financially fit is to claim your gift created just for the buyers of this book. Just go to www.smallbusinessfinancebook.com/kit to sign up for access to your bonus material. Check out smifinancialcoaching.com to learn more about me and the services I offer.

Has this book helped you get your arms around your business finances in at least one area? Great! Please help get the word out to help other small business owners do the same by leaving a review for the book on Amazon. If you have comments and suggestions about the book, please contact me at smifinancialcoaching.com.

References

1. SBA small business survival rate - https://www.sba.gov/sites/default/files/Business-Survival.pdf
2. TD Bank Survey - https://www.entrepreneur.com/article/251252
3. SNL Financial and CNNMoney analysis: http://money.cnn.com/2016/01/14/investing/atm-overdraft-fees/

Glossary of Financial Terms

1099 form: form "used to report a variety of unique income payments to the IRS. This form is usually used when the taxpayer has received income from other sources besides a wage-paying job."

Source: http://www.investinganswers.com/financial-dictionary/tax-center/irs-form-1099-985

Accountant: someone with "a four-year college degree" who "oversee[s] or perform[s] billing, make[s] general ledger entries, review[s] accounts payable activity completed by clerks or technicians or handle[s] payroll."

Source: http://work.chron.com/differences-between-bookkeepers-vs-accountants-vs-cpas-4173.html

Accounts payable: "[u]npaid bills. Accounts that are owed to suppliers (trade creditors) as distinguished from accrued interest, rent, salaries, taxes, and other such accounts."

Source: http://www.businessdictionary.com/definition/accounts-payable-A-P.html

Accounts receivable: "the outstanding invoices a company has or the money the company is owed from its clients. The phrase refers to accounts a business has a right to receive because it has delivered a product or service."

Source: http://www.investopedia.com/terms/a/accountsreceivable.asp

Accrual based accounting: "[a] system of accounting based on the accrual principal, under which revenue is recognized (recorded) when earned, and expenses are recognized when incurred. Totals of revenues and expenses are shown in the financial statements (prepared at the end of an accounting period), whether or not cash was received or paid out in that period."

Source:http://www.businessdictionary.com/definition/accrual-basis-accounting.html

Audit – "an objective examination and evaluation of the financial statements of an organization to make sure that the records are a fair and accurate representation of the transactions they claim to represent."

Source: http://www.investopedia.com/terms/a/audit.asp

Bookkeeper: people who "maintain daily accounting records, posting debits and credits, generating invoices for clients and checks for vendors as well as handling payroll." "[They] typically lack the education of an accountant or CPA, as they gain on-the-job experience."

Source: http://work.chron.com/differences-between-bookkeepers-vs-accountants-vs-cpas-4173.html

Business plan: "a written document that describes in detail how a business, usually a new one, is going to achieve its goals."

Source: http://www.investopedia.com/terms/b/business-plan.asp

C-Corp: "a legal structure that businesses can choose to organize themselves under to limit their owners' legal and financial liabilities."

Source: http://www.investopedia.com/terms/c/c-corporation.asp

CPA: someone who "ha[s] a focused education in accounting and must pass the Uniform Certified Public Accountant Examination." "[B]ecause of their certification, they perform auditing, tax and financial services for individuals, corporations and other business or nonprofit organizations."

Source: http://work.chron.com/differences-between-bookkeepers-vs-accountants-vs-cpas-4173.html

Cash-based accounting: "a major accounting method that recognizes revenues and expenses at the time physical cash is actually received or paid out."

Source: http://www.investopedia.com/terms/c/cashbasis.asp

Cost of Goods Sold (COGS): "the direct costs attributable to the production of the goods sold by a company. This amount includes the cost of the materials used in creating the good along with the direct labor costs used to produce the good."

Source: http://www.investopedia.com/terms/c/cogs.asp

Cost of Sale – "the accumulated total of all costs used to create a product or service, which has been sold."

Source: http://www.accountingtools.com/questions-and-answers/what-is-the-cost-of-sales.html

Deduction – "any item or expenditure subtracted from gross income to reduce the amount of income subject to income tax."

Source: http://www.investopedia.com/terms/d/deduction.asp

Direct cost – "a price that can be completely attributed to the production of specific goods or services."

Source: http://www.investopedia.com/terms/d/directcost.asp

Disability Insurance: "[a] program managed by the Social Security Administration that insures a worker in case of a mishap. Disability insurance offers income protection to individuals who become disabled for a long period of time, and as a result can no longer work during that time period."

Source: http://www.investopedia.com/terms/d/disability-insurance.asp

Distribution – "[a] company's payment of cash, stock or physical products to its shareholders."

Source: http://www.investopedia.com/terms/d/distribution.asp

Doing Business As (DBA): "a legal term meaning that the name under which the business or operation is conducted and presented to the world is not the legal name of the legal person or persons actually owning it and being responsible for it."

Source: http://definitions.uslegal.com/d/dba-or-doing-business-as/

Double-entry system: "a system of accounting in which every transaction has a corresponding positive and negative entry (debits and credits)."

Source: https://debitoor.com/dictionary/double-entry-bookkeeping

Draw – "[t]he withdrawal of business cash or other assets by the owner for the personal use of the owner. Withdrawals of cash by the owner are recorded with a debit to the owner's drawing account and a credit to the cash account."

Source: http://www.accountingcoach.com/terms/D/draw

Employer Identification Number (EIN) – "[a] unique identification number that is assigned to a business entity so that [it] can easily be identified by the Internal Revenue Service. The Employer Identification Number is commonly used by employers for the purpose of reporting taxes."

Source: http://www.investopedia.com/terms/e/employer-identification-number.asp

Expense – "[m]oney spent or cost incurred in an organization's efforts to generate revenue, representing the cost of doing business."

Source: http://www.businessdictionary.com/definition/expense.html

Financial advisor: someone who "provides financial advice or guidance to customers for compensation." [They] "can provide many different services, such as investment management, income tax preparation and estate planning."

Source: http://www.investopedia.com/terms/f/financial-advisor.asp

Financial coach: "a personal finance and/or business expert in areas such as getting out of debt, saving for retirement, budgeting, credit, increasing income, saving for college, avoiding bankruptcy, smart money management and business growth."

Source: http://www.themoneychat.com/financial-coach-vs-financial-advisor/

Fixed Costs: "expenses that have to be paid by a company, independent of any business activity."

Source: http://www.investopedia.com/terms/f/fixedcost.asp

General Liability Insurance: insurance that "protects a business from claims arising from bodily injuries that occur within the workplace, or injuries or damage caused by company employees."

Source: http://www.investopedia.com/terms/l/liability_insurance.asp

Income – "money that an individual or business receives in exchange for providing a good or service or through investing capital."

Source: http://www.investopedia.com/terms/i/income.asp

Invoice – "a commercial document that itemizes a transaction between a buyer and a seller. If goods or services were purchased on credit, the invoice usually specifies the terms of the deal, and provide[s] information on the available methods of payment."

Source: http://www.investopedia.com/terms/i/invoice.asp

LLC (Limited Liability Company): "a corporate structure whereby the members of the company cannot be held personally liable for the company's debts or liabilities."

Source: http://www.investopedia.com/terms/l/llc.asp

Net Profit – "the profit of a company after operating expenses and all other charges including taxes, interest and depreciation have been deducted from total revenue."

Source: http://lexicon.ft.com/Term?term=net-profit

Operating expense: "an expense a business incurs through its normal business operations. Often abbreviated as OPEX, operating expenses include rent, equipment, inventory costs, marketing, payroll, insurance and funds allocated toward research and development."

Source: http://www.investopedia.com/terms/o/operating_expense.asp

Opportunity Cost – "[a] benefit, profit, or value of something that must be given up to acquire or achieve something else."

Source: http://www.businessdictionary.com/definition/opportunity-cost.html

Outsource – to "send[] certain job functions outside a company instead of handling them in house."

Source: https://www.entrepreneur.com/encyclopedia/outsourcing

Overhead – "all ongoing business expenses not including or related to direct labor, direct materials or third-party expenses that are billed directly to customers. A company must pay overhead on an ongoing basis, regardless of whether the company is doing a high or low volume of business."

Source: http://www.investopedia.com/terms/o/overhead.asp

P&L (Profit and Loss Statement): "a financial statement that summarizes the revenues, costs and expenses incurred during a specific period of time, usually a fiscal quarter or year."

Source: http://www.investopedia.com/terms/p/plstatement.asp

Professional Liability Insurance: "Insurance that protects professionals such as accountants, lawyers and physicians against negligence and other claims initiated by their clients."

Source: http://www.investopedia.com/terms/p/professional-liability-insurance.asp

Recordkeeping System – "[s]ystematic procedure by which the records of an organization are created, captured, maintained, and disposed of. This system also ensures their preservation for evidential purposes, accurate and efficient updating, timely availability, and control of access to [] them only by authorized personnel."

Source: http://www.businessdictionary.com/definition/recordkeeping-system.html

Revenue – "the amount of money that a company actually receives during a specific period, including discounts and deductions for returned merchandise."

Source: http://www.investopedia.com/terms/r/revenue.asp

S-Corp: "a form of corporation that meets specific Internal Revenue Code requirements, giving a corporation with 100 shareholders or less the benefit of incorporation while being taxed as a partnership."

Source: http://www.investopedia.com/terms/s/subchapters.asp

Safe harbor – "rules [that] protect[] small businesses from being penalized for the underpayment of current year taxes."

Source: http://smallbusiness.chron.com/safe-harbor-rule-minimum-tax-payments-small-businesses-30859.html

Sales tax: "a tax imposed on retail goods and services at the point of sale."

Source: http://www.accountingtools.com/sales-tax-definition

Schedule C: form used "to report profits or losses from a sole proprietorship."

Source: https://turbotax.intuit.com/tax-tools/tax-tips/Self-Employment-Taxes/-What-is-a-Schedule-C-IRS-form-/INF14443.html

Self-employment tax: "money that a small business owner must pay to the federal government to fund Medicare and Social Security. Self-employment tax is due when an individual has net earnings of $400 or more in self-employment income over the course of the tax year."

Source: http://www.investopedia.com/terms/s/selfemploymenttax.asp

Single-entry system: "a simple form of bookkeeping and accounting in which each financial transaction is recorded with a single entry in a journal or transaction log."

Source: https://www.business-case-analysis.com/single-entry-accounting.html

Social Security Number (SSN) – "a nine-digit number assigned to citizens, some temporary residents and permanent residents in order to track their income and determine benefit entitlements."

Source: http://www.investopedia.com/terms/s/ssn.asp

Sole proprietor: "[s]ole owner of a business; a self-employed person such as a grocer, plumber, or taxi driver. He or she directs the affairs of the enterprise, bears its risks and losses, and takes the profits and benefits."

Source: http://www.businessdictionary.com/definition/sole-proprietor.html

Start up expense: a "[n]on-recurring cost[ ] associated with setting up a business, such as accountant's fees, legal fees, registration charges, as well as advertising, promotional activities, and employee training."

Source: http://www.businessdictionary.com/definition/startup-costs.html

Tax Identification Number (TIN) – "a nine-digit number used as a tracking number by the U.S. Internal Revenue Service (IRS)." "Individuals are assigned TINs in the form of SSNs, whereas businesses such as corporations and partnerships are assigned employer identification numbers (EINs)."

Source: http://www.investopedia.com/terms/t/tax-indentification-number-tin.asp

Use tax: "[a] sales tax on purchases made outside one's state of residence on taxable items that will be used, stored or consumed in one's state of residence and on which no tax was collected in the state of purchase."

Source: http://www.investopedia.com/terms/u/use-tax.asp

Variable Costs: "costs that vary depending on a company's production volume; they rise as production increases and fall as production decreases."

Source: http://www.investopedia.com/terms/v/variablecost.asp

About the Author

Sylvia Inks has built a career on helping companies identify and address the financial fundamentals to building a profitable business. During her ten years with one of the world's largest consulting firms, she worked with Fortune 500 organizations in financial services, insurance, healthcare and technology to improve processes, performance and profitability.

Sylvia now brings that success, experience, and expertise to help small business owners identify, implement, and manage practical, low-stress financial solutions that enable business growth. Viewing her as an invaluable business partner and resource, her clients credit her for giving them hope and a clear path forward. With this book, Sylvia brings her wisdom and expertise to a wider audience.

Sylvia Inks holds a bachelor's degree in business administration from the University of North Carolina at Chapel Hill. She and her husband live with their two sons in North Carolina.

To contact Sylvia, visit SMIFinancialCoaching.com.

A Special Bonus From SMI Financial Coaching

There are books and free information online on how to manage the information and processes needed to run a profitable business, yet in this book I provide all the key topics in one place to give you a great starting point to minimize hours searching for and obtaining this information in various places.

As a special bonus for buying this book, I've created templates to help you get started with getting your arms around your business finances. As an additional bonus, you'll also have access to a resource page with links to not only the resources (companies, software programs, and other resources) mentioned in this book, but also to new tools, technologies, and programs I discover and recommend.

Go to www.smallbusinessfinancebook.com/kit to sign up for access to your bonus material.

As another special gift, I'll also be sending tips, tricks, and great information to make your life easier around your business finances.

To Your Financial Success!

Sylvia

Made in the USA
Middletown, DE
29 January 2017